Macmillan Computer Science Series

Consulting Editor:
Professor F.H. Sumner, University of Manchester

A. Abdellatif, J. Le Bihan, M. Limame, *Oracle - A User's Guide*
Ian O. Angell, *High-resolution Computer Graphics Using C*
Ian O. Angell and Gareth Griffith, *High-resolution Computer Graphics Using FORTRAN 77*
Ian O. Angell and Gareth Griffith, *High-resolution Computer Graphics Using Pascal*
M. Azmoodeh, *Abstract Data Types and Algorithms, second edition*
C. Bamford and P. Curran, *Data Structures, Files and Databases, second edition*
P. Beynon-Davies, *Information Systems Development, second edition*
G.M. Birtwistle, *Discrete Event Modelling on Simula*
Richard Bornat, *Understanding and Writing Compilers*
Linda E.M. Brackenbury, *Design of VLSI Systems - A Practical Introduction*
Alan Bradley, *Peripherals for Computer Systems*
G.R. Brookes and A.J. Stewart, *Introduction to occam2 on the Transputer*
P.C. Capon and P.J. Jinks, *Compiler Engineering Using Pascal*
Robert Cole, *Computer Communications, second edition*
Eric Davalo and Patrick Naïm, *Neural Networks*
S.M. Deen, *Principles and Practice of Database Systems*
C. Delannoy, *Turbo Pascal Programming*
Tim Denvir, *Introduction to Discrete Mathematics for Software Engineering*
D. England *et al.*, *A Sun User's Guide, second edition*
Jean Ettinger, *Programming in C++*
J.S. Florentin, *Microprogrammed Systems Design*
A.B. Fontaine and F. Barrand, *80286 and 90386 Microprocessors*
Michel Gauthier, *Ada - A Professional Course*
M.G. Hartley, M. Healey and P.G. Depledge, *Mini and Microcomputer Systems*
J.A. Hewitt and R.J. Frank, *Software Engineering in Modula-2 - An Object-oriented Approach*
Roger Hutty, *COBOL 85 Programming*
Patrick Jaulent, *The 68000 - Hardware and Software*
M.J. King and J.P. Pardoe, *Program Design Using JSP - A Practical Introduction, second edition*
Bernard Leguy, *Ada - A Programmer's Introduction*
M. Léonard, *Database Design Theory*
David Lightfoot, *Formal Specification Using Z*
A.M. Lister and R.D. Eager, *Fundamentals of Operating Systems, fifth edition*
Elizabeth Lynch, *Understanding SQL*
Tom Manns and Michael Coleman, *Software Quality Assurance, second edition*
B.A.E. Meekings, T.P. Kudrycki and M.D. Soren, *A book on C, third edition*
R.J. Mitchell, *C++ Object-oriented Programming*
R.J. Mitchell, *Microcomputer Systems Using the STE Bus*
R.J. Mitchell, *Modula-2 Applied*
Y. Nishinuma and R. Espesser, *UNIX - First Contact*
Ian Pratt, *Artificial Intelligence*
Pham Thu Quang and C. Chartier-Kastler, *MERISE in Practice*
A.J. Pilavakis, *UNIX Workshop*

continued overleaf

E.J. Redfern, *Introduction to Pascal for Computational Mathematics*
F.D. Rolland, *Programming with VDM*
A.G. Sutcliffe, *Human-Computer Interface Design*
C.J. Theaker and G.R. Brookes, *Concepts of Operating Systems*
M. Thorin, *Real-time Transaction Processing*
M.R. Tolhurst *et al.*, *Open Systems Interconnection*
A.J. Tyrell, *COBOL from Pascal*
I.R. Wilson and A.M. Addyman, *A Practical Introduction to Pascal, second edition*

Other titles
Ian O. Angell and Dimitrios Tsoubelis, *Advanced Graphics on VGA and XGA Cards Using Borland C++*
N. Frude, *A Guide to SPSS/PC+, second edition*
Percy Mett, *Introduction to Computing*
Tony Royce, *COBOL - An Introduction*
Tony Royce, *Structured COBOL - An Introduction*

Programming in C++

Jean Ettinger MSc CEng
School of Computer Science and Information Systems Engineering
University of Westminster

MACMILLAN

First published 1994 by
THE MACMILLAN PRESS LTD
Houndmills, Basingstoke, Hampshire RG21 2XS
and London
Companies and representatives
throughout the world

ISBN 0-333-60682-5

A catalogue record for this book is available
from the British Library.

Printed in Great Britain by Mackays of Chatham PLC

A 3.5 in. MS-DOS diskette containing all the listings of the program
examples is available at the price of £25.00 or $40.00 (inc. postage/
packing - airmail overseas).
Please send your personal cheque to: Globe Book Services Ltd,
Houndmills, Basingstoke, Hampshire, RG21 2XS, UK.
Access/ Visa/ American Express/ Diners Club accepted.
Please quote number and expiry date.
Please quote ISBN 0-333-62295-2 (diskette) when ordering.

To the memory of my husband, Charles,
who always supported my career beyond duty,
and to our excellent teenagers, Andrew and Beth

Contents

Preface

This book has been written to meet the demand for an introductory text explaining the features of the C++ language.

The recent widespread availability of C++ implementations for PCs and Unix systems has encouraged both individuals and businesses to explore its use. Many people coming to these implementations have had no previous programming experience, or have a background in computer languages that have little in common with the structured approach of those in the C++ family of languages.

Moreover, there is a trend to use C++ as a first language for students on computing courses, since it provides a vehicle to introduce many of the current software engineering concepts which aid the production of robust and reusable software.

During the past year, many helpful comments and suggestions for improvements of the material for this text have been made by students studying for BSc computing Degrees, students on an MSc Software Engineering course, and students on several C++ evening Short Courses. A number of these students have been seconded from industry, where many software teams are currently converting to the use of C++ implementations.

There is, as yet, no ANSI standard for C++. AT&T Bell Laboratories are introducing successive versions onto the marketplace. This book discusses C++ in terms of the AT&T version 2.1.

The book assumes no prior knowledge of the earlier C language. All the main features of C++ are discussed, from the beginning, with many program examples to illustrate them. Exercises are provided, and all of the programs that they suggest can be developed on any C++ implementation compatible with the AT&T version 2.1 or above.

Readers with a knowledge of C should note that only Chapter 3, on the structure statements, contains no new features for a C programmer. There are small differences, as well as the more obvious larger ones, between the two languages. Such readers should scan Chapters 2, 4, 5, and 6 noting the smaller differences between the languages. Chapter 9 shows that C++ provides easier ways of allocating and deallocating memory dynamically than C. Some parts of the C language have been omitted, since they were not essential to this introductory overview of C++, even though they have been inherited by C++.

All implementations of C++ include ANSI C libraries. This gives a common core to all C++ programming. For this reason, the program examples and exercises use only these libraries, and deal only with numerical and text (character, string) handling.

Most screen-handling facilities, and specialist input facilities such as those for a mouse, are provided with further C++ and/or C libraries specific to the implementation. For example, Borland Turbo C++ provides ObjectWindows, which make use of the MicroSoft Windows environment, to enable a programmer to create a Windows interface for an application program.

Appendix 1 gives details of entering, compiling, linking, and making C++ programs using either Unix with GNU C++ or Borland Turbo C++ for PCs.

My thanks to my students, to my colleagues, J. A. Bermudez and Alan Lake, and to my publisher Malcolm J. Stewart at Macmillan, for their encouragement and corrections to this text. All the remaining mistakes are my own!

Jean Ettinger
University of Westminster
EMail: ettingj@uk.ac.westminster

1 The inheritance of C++

C++ is a recent programming language developed to exploit some of the latest *software engineering* methodologies that aim to make software easier to develop, easier to enlarge, and as reliable as possible. It is an enhanced and extended form of one of the major *structured*, *imperative*, languages, C, using features first found in related languages such as Simula, Pascal, and Ada, and features found in *object-oriented programming* languages.

The first version of C++ was developed by Bjarne Stroustrup in the AT&T Bell Laboratories in the early 1980s and released in 1985. It immediately aroused much interest and, within a year, had been implemented on more than 20 different hardware systems, from home microcomputers to mainframes.

Since then, further versions have been released by AT&T. An ANSI C++ committee has been established, but has not yet produced a standard at the time of publication.

This chapter shows how C++ has *inherited* features from other languages. C++ is not just 'a bigger, later C': the C++ language description modifies C in both small and large ways, incorporating and developing software features from other languages as well.

1.1 The Algol family of computer languages

C++ is one of the latest member of the Algol family of languages. All of these languages are *imperative* languages which essentially enable a task to be performed by giving a set of sequential commands to a computer. These commands are known as *statements*.

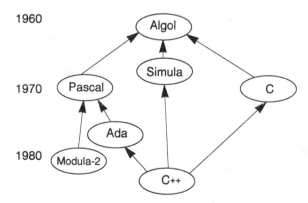

An inheritance diagram for the Algol family of languages
The arrows point from a derived language to a base language

1

The inheritance diagram for the Algol family of languages is simplified, and omits less well known languages. Nonetheless, we can deduce from it many of the main characteristics of C++. Inheritance here does not imply that a 'child' language inherits all the characteristics of a 'parent' language, but it does inherit some. The following brief descriptions of languages introduce features of C++ that are derived from preceding members of its family of languages.

1.1.1 Algol

Algol (1960) was the first language to enable a *structured flow of program control* (*goto anywhere* statements were strongly discouraged). Algol provided *structure statements* such as:

> if (*condition true*) do *something1* else *something2*.

Algol also provided *procedures* whereby program control, at any point, can be passed to a procedure (a section of code elsewhere) that performs a subtask of the overall program task; when the subtask is completed program control returns to the point where the procedure was called. In C++ we will refer to procedures as *functions*.

1.1.2 Pascal

Pascal is a *strongly-typed* language, as are Ada and Modula-2. For programs in such languages, the types of all data objects are known by the time the program is translated and *the compiler checks that data objects are used properly with operators and passed to procedures with the correct types.*

Pascal has a predefined set of types of data objects. These types are known to the compiler which also knows the operations that can be used with objects of a specific type. The types include *integer* (positive and negative whole numbers), *real* (numbers including a fractional part such as 4.37 and −0.001), *char* (alphanumeric, digit, punctuation, and control characters), *array* (lists of data objects where each can be selected by their position in the lists), *record* (groups of logically related data objects), *pointer* (to hold addresses in memory of data objects), and *file* (usually a text file, holding data).

1.1.3 C - the most influential 'parent'

C was developed as a language for writing systems software: software that enables programmers to make full and easy use of the hardware of a computer. It was first used to develop the Unix operating system.

The C language has become one of the most important programming languages during the last twenty years. Its strength comes from combining the advantages of a high-level language with the flexibility and efficiency of a machine-level language.

A C compiler does not have to check that a data object is being handled correctly (the language is *weakly-typed*), and it is easy to make run-time errors that would not occur with programs written in most of the other languages mentioned here.

It is a relatively small language, and can be implemented without difficulty on most computers. Much of the software recently developed for PCs has been written in C. It has become a 'general-purpose' language.

C has essentially two predefined types: **integer** and **float** (real numbers). Objects of these types are handled by operators such as the arithmetic operators +, -, * and /, and the relational operators >, > =, <, < = , = = (equal) and ! = (not equal). C++ has the same predefined types, and operators.

C++ also has the same structure statement formats as C.

C++ implementations are usually provided with the ANSI C standard libraries, which define many useful functions for handling subtasks that are frequently performed. C++ adds the **iostream** library to the C libraries, which is used for input and output.

Most C++ compilers will also compile C program code. Files of program code written in C can be linked to a C++ program.

1.1.4 Simula - the most influential 'grandparent'

One of the first application areas to which 'high-level' computer languages were applied was that of the simulation of discrete systems such as airports, docks, or garages with petrol pumps on the forecourt. These systems were simulated on computers to determine the number of runways that should be provided, the number of docking bays for ships, or the number of petrol pumps required.

If we consider airport systems, then we know that they might handle Boeing 747s as well as small 2-seater planes. We can describe an aeroplane in general terms: its *data members* such as engines and doors, and its *member procedures* such as taking off, flight path, landing.

In Norway in the early 1960s, the simulation language Simula was developed to describe and simulate such systems by examining the 'life cycle' of data objects within the system. Thus an optimal solution could be reached before construction started. Norway has used Simula to find the best solution for many of its state developments over a number of years.

Simula was based on Algol with the addition of the **class** concept. Using this concept, it is possible to define a class (for example, the class of aeroplanes) and generate objects of that class (for example, 6 Boeing 747s and 2 small planes). It is this concept that was inherited by some later languages, including C++, so much so that C++ could even be described as a modern version of Simula.

This notion, that the type (class) of a set of data objects, and the operations that handle these data objects belong together, is the basis for the idea of an *abstract data type*. We can define an abstract 'aeroplane', and then declare and use actual objects of type 'aeroplane' (for example, Boeing1, ..., small1, ...).

1.1.5 Ada

The development of Ada was sponsored by the US Department of Defense in the middle 1970s. It required a standard language to be used in embedded computer systems that control part of a larger system such as a missile, an aircraft, or a production-line.

Although Ada is based on Pascal in many respects, it is much larger and includes the idea of a *package*. An Ada package is often defined in a separate library. A library consists of two files: a definition file giving the types provided by the package and the procedures available to handle objects of these types, and an implementation file that contains the full details of how these types and procedures are implemented. These packages aid *information hiding*, because the details of an implementation are hidden from the user who may only access a library through its definition file.

Ada allows the user to build up libraries of packages that have been debugged, so that the packages may be reused with later programs. Also, within a programming team, each team member may be allocated to the development of a separate package; what each package should provide for the overall software task is known through its library definition file, but the other team members are not concerned with the implementation.

Ada allows the development of generic (**template**) procedures and packages. These are subprograms or packages that provide a 'template' from which actual procedures or packages may be defined with much in common, but also with individual small differences as required. The specific definition required at a point in the program code is determined by the compiler. We could consider a generic package for 'aeroplane' from which we could obtain the actual package needed for 'Boeings' or for 'small 2-seater planes'.

Ada also enables the *overloading* of procedures. This allows several definitions of a procedure to be made. The specific definition of a procedure required at a point in the program code is determined by the compiler, at translation time, from the types of the data items that the procedure handles. (This form of binding a procedure definition is known as *early* or *static binding*.) An analogy for this may be found by considering the procedure of 'landing' which we could use for both a 'Boeing' and a 'small 2-seater plane', but which would be defined slightly differently for each ('Boeings' need a longer runway ...).

1.2 Smalltalk, an object-oriented language

Smalltalk has been the main language for developing programs using only the object-oriented programming methodology.

Programmers are provided with a base class definition and can derive *hierarchies of class definitions* from this suitable for a particular application. *Objects* of a class can be created.

A class definition contains *methods* for handling objects of that class.

A program consists of a series of *messages* sent to objects. *Objects respond to a message in different ways*, since a message is implemented by a method defined in the class of the object to which a message is sent. Which method is used is determined when the program is run. The binding of the definition of the method to the code at run-time is called *late binding* or *dynamic binding*.

This concept, that 'objects respond to a message in different ways' is known as *polymorphism*, and is a key concept, together with that of the *inheritance of class definitions*, in object-oriented programming.

The object-oriented programming methodology encourages the programmer to concentrate on the classes (types) of the objects being handled by an application program. It may be that class definitions already exist for many of these objects. These definitions should be used. It is likely that suitable class definitions can be derived from existing ones, and are therefore relatively easy to develop.

Once the classes of the objects used in the application have been established, and the methods exist to handle these objects as required, the application software can then be written with all the tools to hand.

1.3 An overview of C++

C++, the language to be discussed much further in this book, derives many features from other languages in its 'family'. The inheritance diagram used to show the derivation of C++ from earlier languages is in the same format, and has much the same implication, as the inheritance diagrams used to show the connections between derived and base classes in C++.

C++ derives structure statement forms and functions via C from Algol. So the *structured programming methodology* can be used to develop program code and ensure that software always executes in an ordered manner.

It should be noted that there are some changes in function handling whereby C++ provides for the definition of **inline** functions and for the passing of arguments to functions by reference as well as by value.

C++ inherits the predefined data types and operator definitions for data objects of these types from C. It also inherits its derived types from C, but adding the *reference* type.

It inherits the class concept via Ada from Simula, so that users can define their own data type as a **class** that can include the definitions of functions to handle data objects of that class. C++ goes further than Ada in allowing most operators as well as functions to be overloaded by the programmer, so that the action of an operator symbol can be redefined when an operand is a class object.

User-defined libraries can be developed. Each library is usually made up from two files: a header file and an implementation file. Once developed and debugged, these libraries can be reused whenever necessary. Class definitions are usually placed in a library which enables abstraction.

C++ has taken the concept of **templates** from Ada, but there is not an agreed standard implementation of all aspects of these at the current time.

C++ also enables programmers to develop software using the *object-oriented programming methodology*. Derived classes may be defined that inherit all the features of one or more base classes and can redefine, or add to, these features. *Hierarchies of classes* can be developed, where a derived class may have *multiple inheritance* from several base classes.

Further, C++ is more strongly typed than C. In particular, the compiler checks the types of the actual arguments passed to a function to determine, in many cases, the specific function definition to be inserted into the program code at a function call (*static binding*). It is not, however, so strongly typed as Pascal and Ada. For example, the lack of range checking for objects of the predefined types can lead to the occasional run-time error, an illustration of which is given in Chapter 4. (Chapter 8 shows how the redefinition of a type as a class can overcome such a problem.)

This slight 'weakness' allows C++ to implement **virtual** functions within a hierarchy of classes. These are member functions with several associated definitions where the specific definition to be used is determined at run-time (*dynamic binding*), rather than by the compiler. These virtual functions are equivalent to the methods of Smalltalk. Selecting a virtual function has the same effect as the sending of a message in Smalltalk: the response depends on the class of the object being used to select the function. So the further feature of object-oriented languages, *polymorphism*, is also enabled by this language.

C++ allows the programmer to combine the conventional, structured programming methodology with the object-oriented programming methodology. It is hoped that, in this way, programmers can 'get the best of both worlds' in which to develop large software systems.

Programmers using C++ should first utilise the object-oriented methodology and consider the classes (types) of the objects used in an application and the methods (ways) in which these objects will be used in that application. Definitions for the classes should then be found, or derived, or developed. Each method is written as a function using the structured programming methodology to ensure that the sequence of actions in the implementation of the method is correct.

Once the classes of the objects in the application have been established and fully defined, the application program is written using structured programming to ensure, once again, that the sequence of actions taken when the program is run is correct.

Exercises for Chapter 1

1. You are asked to help with the design of a simulation of a new superstore that is to be built where the optimal number of point-of-sale terminals has to be determined.

Describe different classes of objects that will be used in the simulation and, for each class, suggest some ways (methods) in which objects of that class can be handled.

2. You are asked to help with the design of a graphics library to be supplied with a software package.

Describe different classes of objects that could be provided in the library and, for each class, suggest some methods for handling objects of that class.

Can any of the classes be made to relate to each other? Give some suggestions for possible derivations of some classes from other classes.

2 Simple programs, and the predefined data types

We first consider simple programs that demonstrate how the **iostream** library is used to output text *strings*, and to input and output whole numbers and numbers with fractional parts.

These numbers are data objects of the *predefined types*. Their storage requirements in memory, and the operators that are used to handle them, are already defined within the C++ compiler.

This chapter introduces *type conversion* methods for changing objects from one type to another. It also shows how standard library functions can be used to perform subtasks of an overall program task.

2.1 The first program

We begin with the traditional first program in a new language - writing out the message *Hello, world!* onto the standard output device, usually a screen:

```
// file hello writes out a message
#include <iostream.h>
                        // include this header file for I/O
void main( )
{
   cout << "Hello, world!\n";
                   // output message with a newline finish
}
```

2.1.1 Comments

A *comment* is ignored by the compiler. We use comments to help *document* a program, to make it more understandable. The heading comments give the file name, and an overall description of the program task.

Comments are usually enclosed by // and the *end-of-the-line*.

Comments can also be enclosed by /* and */. These enclosures are useful for comments that are more than one line in length, and also if we want the compiler to ignore several lines of program code when, for example, we are *debugging* - searching for the source of a program error.

2.1.2 Header files and the #include directive

Almost all our programs will require input from the keyboard and output to a screen, and so almost all our programs will need to make use of the *iostream library* facilities. The **iostream.h** *header file* is inserted at the beginning of a program with the **#include** *directive*.

The first step in compiling a C++ program is carried out by the *pre-processor*; directives are commands to this preprocessor. All preprocessor directives begin with the symbol **#**. Preprocessing is carried out before compilation, before a program is translated.

The **#include** <iostream.h> directive makes the preprocessor insert (paste) all of the iostream.h header file into the program at the point where the directive occurs. The header files of libraries provided with a C++ implementation are always enclosed within the angle brackets, < and >, when used with this directive.

2.1.3 A C++ program consists of one or more functions

A program must contain a *main function* where execution always starts. **main** is the main function identifier, and the parentheses, (and), following **main** indicate to the compiler that it is a function.

We enclose the *body* of a function in the curly braces { and }. These braces enclose the sequence of statements whose actions enable the function to carry out its task. Each statement within this sequence is concluded with a semi-colon ;

Later, we will learn how to write other functions, and functions with *arguments* that are passed within the parentheses.

The keyword **void**[1] used before **main( )** indicates that no value is returned by the function.

2.1.4 Text strings and escape sequences

The double quotes " " are used to enclose a sequence of characters: a *string constant* (or *string literal*).

\n, at the end of the string *Hello, world!*, represents a single character: it is the *escape sequence* for the *newline* character (RETURN or ENTER key). Other escape sequences that may be used in a string can be found in Appendix 2.

Text characters within a string are usually from the ASCII character set. This set is also given in Appendix 2.

2.2 Introduction to input and output using the iostream library

In C++, input is read from, and output is written to, *streams*. When **iostream.h** is included in a program module, several standard streams are defined automatically.

---

[1]A return-type of **void** is required for the C++ **main( )** function with MS-DOS and MicroSoft Windows implementations. On C++ Unix implementations, **void** should be omitted and may be replaced by **int**.

The stream **cin** is used for the standard input stream, normally from the keyboard; the stream **cout** is used for the standard output stream, normally sent to the screen[2].

In this program we have output a single text string to the screen. We have *inserted* the string into the output stream **cout**.

2.2.1 The insertion operator << is used to put an object into an output stream

The *insertion operator* << inserts data into an output stream. It takes two operands: the left operand is an output stream object, and the right operand is the data object to be output. The C++ implementation can output data objects of all of the predefined types; definitions of the operator for each of these types of operands are held in the iostream library.

A series of << operators can be used to output several data values within a single statement (but notice that no spaces, or other separators, will be inserted unless we specify them). The operator is used before each of the objects that are to be inserted into the output stream. For example, we could have written out the message and newline character using the statement:

```
cout << "Hello, world!" << '\n';
```
where single quotes are used to enclose just one character.

The output stream **cout** is *buffered*: values inserted into **cout** are not written directly to an output device, instead they are placed in temporary storage called a *buffer*. When the buffer is full, its contents are output in a single operation.

2.2.2 The iostream manipulators

Manipulators can be used to carry out operations on these buffered streams. The set of iostream manipulators is given in Appendix 5.

The example programs will often use the **endl** manipulator. This *inserts a newline* and then *flushes* the buffer - it outputs the contents of the buffer even if it is not full. So we can rewrite the statement to output the string and then a 'newline' character in the first program as:

```
cout << "Hello, world!" << endl ;
```
Manipulators that take arguments use the **iomanip** library. The example program in 2.7.1 shows the use of one such manipulator, **setprecision**, that takes an argument.

---

[2]Both the Unix and DOS operating systems allow this I/O to be redirected using the < or > operators in the program execution command line so that other streams (files) can hold the standard input and/or the standard output for a program. Microsoft Windows does not allow redirection.

2.2.3 The extraction operator >> takes an object from an input stream

The extraction operator >> also has several definitions, known to the compiler, which enable it to be used to read data objects of the predefined types.

These operators are overloaded, which means that they each have several definitions. The compiler chooses which definition to use by looking at the *operands* of the operator.

The extraction operator will read in a predefined data object until it meets 'white space' such as ' ' (space), '\t' (tab), or '\n' (newline), or, for **char** objects, it just reads in a single (non-white space) character. (There is a manipulator for reading 'white space'.)

The use of **cin** flushes the buffer for **cout** automatically.

2.3 Identifiers

We give *identifiers* (names) to objects and functions (and, later, to classes). An identifier can consist of letters, digits, and the underline character '_' .

The first character of an identifier must be a letter character or the underline character '_'. Avoid beginning or ending identifiers with _ (underline) because the implementation will probably use such identifiers for specific purposes.

An identifier should not be a C++ *keyword* (see Appendix 3).

A C++ compiler is *case-sensitive* which means that it distinguishes between upper-case and lower-case letters. So the identifiers count, Count, and COUNT, for example, are all regarded as different from each other.

2.4 The predefined data types

C++ inherits its predefined types from C. These are the integer (whole number) types, and the fractional number types (numbers such as 3.45, -0.003).

The definition and storage requirement for data objects of each of these types is known to the compiler, as are the definitions for the operators to handle objects of these types such as the arithmetic operators +, -, *, and /, the relational operators <, <=, == (equal), != (not equal), >=, and >, and the logical operators && (AND), || (OR), and ! (NOT).

Like many other languages, C++ requires an object to have its *type* given before it is used: the compiler can then allocate the correct amount of storage to the object. Since the definitions of the predefined types are known to the compiler, we only need to *declare* our requirements of storage of objects of these types when we need a new one.

2.5 Declarations, initialisations, constants

Declarations request and obtain storage space for an *identified* object, and can also initialise the value of that object.

Declarations can be made at any point within our program (unlike many other languages which only allow declarations to be made at the top of a program or at the beginning of a function).

An object can be *initialised* when it is declared - given an initial value.

When an object is declared to be a **const**ant its value cannot be changed during program execution. A data item that is to be a constant value has its declaration prefixed by the keyword **const**.

2.6 The predefined integer types

In ascending order of size, the main predefined integer types are **char, int,** and **long int**. Each of these types can be modified to define only objects with unsigned values by placing the keyword **unsigned** in front of the type.

In this book all numerical values will be decimal values[3].

char objects are *characters* (usually from the ASCII character set). They are each stored in a *byte* (8 bits). Arithmetic is not carried out directly on objects of type **char**: when a **char** appears in an arithmetic expression, it is implicitly converted to type **int** before any arithmetic operations are applied to it.

char constants are placed within single quotation marks, for example, 'A', '9', '?', ' ' (space), and '\0' (null) are all of type **char**.

int objects are integers, often held in 2 bytes on PCs when the range would be from -2^{15} to $+(2^{15} - 1)$.

unsigned int objects then have a range from 0 to $+(2^{16} - 1)$.

long int objects are integers, often held in 4 bytes on PCs when the range is from -2^{31} to $+ (2^{31} - 1)$.

unsigned long int objects then have the range from 0 to $+(2^{32} - 1)$.

It should be noted that a C++ compiler does not check whether an object of these types is within the range for an implementation; it is easily possible to perform a calculation and inadvertently obtain an incorrect result.

Further, these types will have different ranges on different systems!

2.6.1 Integers, the unary + and - operators and the arithmetic operators

A *unary* operator has one operand. Applying the + and - unary operators to integers makes them *signed integers*, as in +14, -64.

A *binary* operator has two operands. The arithmetic operators are binary operators. For integers, the arithmetic operators are + (addition), - (subtraction), * (multiplication), / (division, but giving the integer part of the result only), and % (modulus, giving the remainder after division).

---

[3]A leading **0** digit indicates to the compiler that a numerical value is *octal*, and leading **0x** indicates that a numerical value is *hexadecimal*.

Operators are used to form *expressions* within statements. For example, if a program makes the declaration of an **int** object and gives it the initial value of **6**:

```
int number = 6;
```

then the expression

```
number / 4
```

evaluates to **1** since the result of a division with integer operands is an integer, and the expression

```
number % 2
```

evaluates to **0**, the remainder after the division of **number** by **2**.

The parentheses (and) can be used to alter the *precedence* of the operators within an expression, so the expression

```
4 * number - 1
```

evaluates to **23** (since * has a higher precedence than -), but the expression

```
4 * ( number - 1 )
```

evaluates to **20** (since the operation within the parentheses is performed first).

2.6.2 A simple integer handling program

```
/* file integer reads in an integer and then writes out
                                        its square */
#include <iostream.h>
void main( )
{
   int number;                     // declaring an integer

   cout << "What number do you want to square?: ";
   cin >> number;                  // reading in an integer

   cout << "\nSquare of " << number
           << " is " << number * number << endl;
              // outputting text, integers, and a newline
}
```

Note that in this program, the **iostream** insertion operator < < is used before each different *type* of data object to be output. Here we are outputting text *strings*, *integer values*, and a *manipulator*. Each data object requires a different definition of the operator.

An integer value is read in from the keyboard using the statement

```
cin >> number;
```

The operands of this extraction operator are **cin** (the standard input stream) and the integer **number**. When this statement is executed, the program 'waits' for the user to enter an integer.

When this program is run, make sure that the value of the expression

```
number * number
```

does not exceed the maximum integer on your implementation - an incorrect answer or an aborted program will be obtained if it is too large!

2.7 The predefined types for fractional numbers

These types are for 'real' decimal numbers that explicitly contain a decimal point, for example, the number 1.52.

float and **double** are the main 'floating-point' predefined types. These types differ in the *accuracy* (the number of correct decimal digits) of their representation of decimal numbers.

float data objects are normally stored in 4 bytes (IEEE single-precision), and will have approximately 7 accurate decimal digits.

double objects are normally stored in 8 bytes (IEEE double-precision), and will have approximately 17 accurate decimal digits.

For these numbers, the arithmetic operators are +, -, * (multiplication), and / (division).

When displaying a fractional number, its precision may be set using the manipulator **setprecision(i)** where the **integer** argument **i** is the number of digits required after the decimal point. To use this manipulator that takes an argument, the **iomanip.h** header file must be included.

2.7.1 A simple fractional numbers handling program

```
/* file real converts a Fahrenheit value to Centigrade,
            the result will have three decimal digits
                        after the decimal point */
#include <iostream.h>
#include <iomanip.h>

void main( )
{
    const double multiplier = 5.0 / 9.0;
                        /* declaring and initialising
        a constant object multiplier of type double */
    double fah;
        // declares an unintialised double object fah

    cout << "Give a Fahrenheit temperature value: ";
    cin >> fah;
    double cent = multiplier * ( fah - 32 );
                    // declaring and initialising cent

    cout << "The corresponding Centigrade value is: "
        << setprecision( 3 ) << cent << endl;
}
```

Note that in this program, **multiplier** has been assigned the value of **5.0 / 9.0** to ensure that the correct fractional value is obtained from the division. If the fraction is written as **5 / 9**, an **integer** division is performed giving the integer result of **0**, and hence making all the **cent** values equal to **0** as well!

The program also illustrates *implicit type conversion* (see 2.9). When the following expression is evaluated

```
fah - 32
```

the **integer 32** is promoted to a **double** before it is subtracted from **fah**.

So C++ allows the mixing of the predefined data types in expressions, but care needs to be taken to ensure that the required results are always obtained.

2.8 The assignment, compound assignment, and sizeof operators

We have already met the insertion, extraction, and arithmetic operators. C++ provides many more operators - the full list of the operators is given in Appendix 4 which also shows each operator's precedence and associativity. These operators will be introduced, as necessary, during this and the following chapters.

Operators and operands form *expressions* which can be part of a statement or a statement in their own right - an *expression statement*. An *expression statement* is formed by an expression concluded with a semi-colon ;

Input and output statements, such as

```
cin >> number;
```

are expression statements.

2.8.1 The assignment operator

Assignment is an operation in C++. The operator symbol = does not imply equality but that the value of the right-hand operand becomes the new value of the left-hand operand. *Normally, only the right-hand operand may be itself an expression.*

In the previous program example, there is an expression that initialises **cent**:

```
cent = multiplier * ( fah - 32 )
```

where the right-hand expression is evaluated first, and then its value is assigned to **cent**.

The left-hand operand of an assignment expression is known as an *lvalue.*

For the assignment operator, *the value of the right-hand operand becomes the value of the assignment expression itself.*

Examples of expressions and expression statements using the assignment operator
If the following declaration statement has been made:

```
int i, j;
```

declaring two unintialised integers, then the expression

```
i = 1
```

has itself the value of **1** and also assigns the value of **1** to **i**;
and the expression statement, concluding with a semi-colon,

```
i = 1;
```

has the value of **1** and also assigns the value of **1** to **i**.

The following expression statement
```
j = i = 1;
```
is evaluated as
```
j = ( i = 1 );
```
where the right-hand expression is evaluated first to give **1**, and this value is then assigned to **j**.

This last expression statement example shows the *associativity* of the assignment operator. The assignment operator has the associativity of *right to left*. So **j** is associated with (**i = 1**), the latter expression is hence evaluated first giving a value of **1** which is then finally assigned to **j**.

If you are not certain about the precedence and associativity of operators (and who is?), use parentheses (brackets) to make sure that operators and operands are grouped together as you require!

2.8.2 The compound assignment operators

Assignment is used very frequently with the arithmetic operators. C++ provides *compound assignment* operators which are terse, abbreviated forms of simple combinations of these operators.

For example, if **i** and **j** have been declared as integers or fractional numbers, then the statement
```
i = i + j ;
```
can be written in a 'shorthand' form as
```
i += j ;
```

The following list shows the set of these operators:

abbreviated form	unabbreviated form	
i += j ;	**i = i + j ;**	// **i** and **j** can be integer or fractional
i -= j ;	**i = i - j ;**	// **i** and **j** can be integer or fractional
i *= j ;	**i = i * j ;**	// **i** and **j** can be integer or fractional
i /= j ;	**i = i / j ;**	// **i** and **j** can be integer or fractional
i %= j ;	**i = i % j ;**	// **i** and **j** can only be integer

2.8.3 The sizeof operator gives the storage requirements of a data object

This can be a useful operator to find out the number of bytes given to store an object. It can be used to find the storage requirements of an object given by the *identifier* of the object; alternatively, it can be used, as in the program below, to find out the number of bytes of storage allocated to objects of a certain type given by the *type identifier*.

It is a unary operator where the identifier is placed in parentheses to the right of the operator.

```
/* file size finding the size (and hence range) of
                             numbers of different types */
#include <iostream.h>
void main( )
{
   cout << "Integers need: " << sizeof( int )
         << " bytes" << endl;
   cout << "Chars need: " << sizeof( char )
         << " bytes" << endl;
   cout << "Doubles need: " << sizeof( double )
         << " bytes" << endl;
}
```
The output given by this program will differ between implementations.

2.9 Type conversions

We frequently need to change values from one data type to another. Converting an object to a type with a wider range of values or to a greater degree of precision is easy and straightforward, but it should be noted that it is equally easy to change in the reverse manner and obtain unexpected results!

Type conversions can be *implicit* (carried out automatically) or *explicit* (specifically requested by the programmer).

2.9.1 Implicit type conversions (promotions) of objects of the predefined types

As we have seen, C++ allows *mixed mode expressions* in which the operands may have different data types. Before an operation is carried out with such operands, one operand is converted to the data type of the other. Essentially, the operand with the 'smaller' data type is converted into the 'larger' data type, the promotions ranking in the order of ascending size:

char, int, unsigned int, long int, unsigned long int, float, double
The operand with the data type that comes first in this list is converted to the type that comes second.

2.9.2 Explicit type conversions

C++ provides two methods in which a programmer can specify explicitly when a conversion should take place. The first way is to use the *type cast operator* (as in C), the second way (only in C++) is to use *the specified type in a function-call notation*.

The first method uses the *type cast operator* to enclose the specified type in parentheses before the operand; for example, the expression

```
( double ) 1066
```
changes the **integer** value to a **double** value.

Note that the *type cast operator* can be seen in Appendix 4 as *(type)* at the same level of precedence as the other unary operators.

The alternative method of converting a type is to use the type identifier as a function identifier with the operand to be converted in parentheses as an argument as, for example, in the expression

```
double ( 1066 )
```

Although this may seem the more reasonable way, there are some circumstances where it cannot be used, so we are allowed both of these conversion methods. The example program given in 5.1.4 shows the use of explicit type conversions.

2.10 Data objects

This chapter has described data items as *objects*. Objects may have *variable* values or *constant* values and may, or may not, have identifiers.

An *object* is a region of memory in which a value (or values) can be stored; it is characterised by the address of that memory, its name (if any), its type, and the value(s) associated with it.

Its *address* is that of the memory that the object occupies. We are hardly ever interested in the actual numerical value of the address of that memory (except, possibly, in hardware control applications which are beyond the scope of this book). C++ provides *pointers* to hold memory addresses. Pointers hold the addresses of objects. Pointers are discussed further in Chapter 4.

An object may have zero or more *names*. These may be identifiers, or may be more complex (an object which is a component of an array **vector** may be referred to as **vector[6]**, for example).

The *type* of a data object determines the type(s) of the value(s) that can be stored in the object. The type determines the size of the corresponding region of memory, and defines the operations with which the object can be used in an expression. The compiler contains the definitions for the predefined types and for the derived types discussed in Chapter 4. We shall see that *classes* are user-defined types.

The *value* of an object is the bit pattern that is stored in the corresponding region of memory. How that bit pattern is understood depends on the type of the object.

2.11 Using libraries

A number of libraries are provided with each implementation. Usually these include the ANSI C libraries; often there are other libraries as well which may be specific to the operating system and environment of the implementation.

By *including* the library header file, we can make use of the functions and other definitions provided by a library.

2.11.1 Program using a random number generator function from stdlib

This program **includes** the header file for the **stdlib** library as well as that for the **iostream** library. From the **stdlib** library the function **rand( )** is used, which will produce a random integer from the set generated by **srand( )**.

The function **srand( )** will give different random number(s) on each execution run if it is given a new *seed* on each run. (Often the seed is taken from a **time** given from the computer's clock, thus giving a new value for each execution run of the program; this program just requests an integer value.)

RAND_MAX is defined in **stdlib.h**, and has the value of the largest random integer for the implementation.

```
// file randnumb using stdlib library definitions
#include <iostream.h>
#include <stdlib.h>
void main( )
{
   int seed;
   cout << "Random numbers are from 0 to "
          << RAND_MAX << endl;
   cout << "Input a seed to generate new numbers: ";
   cin >> seed;
   srand( seed );              // random numbers generated
   cout << "Random number is " << rand( ) << endl;
              // output first random number in this set
}
```

Exercises for Chapter 2

1. Write a program to output a message including two escape sequences.

2. Use the **sizeof** operator to find the number of bytes used to store objects of the types **char**, **int, long int, float,** and **double** on the computer that you are using.

3. Write a program that will input an **integer** number, and then output the **integer** value obtained when the number has been divided by 3. Test the program several times with varying **integers**. Include in the test data input **integers** that are not exactly divisible by 3. What do you deduce about the division of an **integer** by an **integer**?

4. Write a program that will input an **integer** number, convert the **integer** number into a number of type **float**, divide the **float** number by 3 and output the result. This example shows that numbers of different types can be used in an arithmetic expression. Output the result firstly as a **float**, and then as an **integer**.

5. Write a program that will input an amount of money in British pounds and pence, and then output the corresponding value of that amount in USA dollars and cents. Since the exchange rate between the two currencies continually fluctuates, this rate also needs to be input.

6. **Include** the **math.h** header file of the **math** library, and write a program that will read in two **double** numbers, x and y, and then output "x to the power of y". The **math** function **pow(x, y)** will give the result as another **double** number.

7. **Include** the **float.h** header file of the **float** library, and write a program to find the number of decimal digits of accuracy of **float** and **double** numbers on the computer that you are using by writing the values of **FLT_DIG** and **DBL_DIG**, which are defined in **float.h**.

8. Input an **integer**, in the usual way, as a decimal number. Use the manipulators **oct** and **hex** from the **iostream** library to output it first as an octal value and then as a hexadecimal value.

9. The **iomanip** library enables the manipulators which take arguments. Include the **iomanip.h** header file so that the set of digits, 0, 1, 2, 3, 4, can be output on a single line, each with a field-width of 6 and the spaces between the digits filled with the * character. Use manipulators **setw(6)** and **setfill('*')** in the output statement.

3 Structured programming

Languages that enable the development of programs using the structured programming methodology provide a set of *structure statements*, so that choices can be made about which sequence of statements are to be executed and so that sequences of statements can be repeated. These structure statements are used for *selection (alternation, choice)*, and *repetition (iteration, looping)*.

In structured programing, the *flow of control* of program execution is ordered, and **goto** *anywhere* statements are not used:

◇ program execution passes from one statement to the next,

◇ each statement has one entry point and one exit point,

◇ one or more statements may be nested inside a structure statement.

The *layout* of a program should clearly show the flow of program execution. The sequences of statements within the selection and repetition structure statements are indented (using the TAB key) to show that they are internal to such a statement.

All the example programs in Chapter 2 contained just one *sequence* of statements within the **main( )** function block, where:

◇ a single statement is concluded with a semi-colon ;

◇ a *block* of statements in sequence is enclosed by the braces, { and }

A *block* of statements in sequence is also known as a *compound statement*.

Before we look at the C++ selection and repetition statements, we need to consider how C++ represents the Boolean values of *true* and *false*, and how Boolean expressions (evaluating to true or false) can be formed using the relational and logical operators.

3.1 Boolean values, boolean expressions

The two Boolean values are *true* and *false*. Essentially, at the hardware level, computers are based on *Boolean algebra* which is the logical manipulation of two-state items. We do not discuss Boolean algebra further here: our introductory programs will use simple and obvious logic!

Unlike some other languages, C++ does not have a Boolean data type, but uses type **int**, so:

◇ *false* is represented by the **integer** value 0

◇ *true* is represented by any non-zero **integer** value (often 1).

3.1.1 Boolean expressions

Boolean expressions give either the result *true* (1, non-zero) or the result *false* (zero). They are used as *control expressions* in selection and repetition structure statements.

Boolean expressions are usually formed using the *relational* and the *logical* operators. These operators produce either 1 (*true*) or 0 (*false*) as their result; the operands need not be 0 or 1, any non-zero operand will be treated as *true* and a zero operand will be treated as *false*.

3.1.2 The relational operators

The relational operators are:

==	equals (two adjacent = symbols),	!=	not equal to,
<=	less than or equal to,	<	less than,
>=	greater than or equal to,	>	greater than.

Remember that parentheses (brackets) are useful to ensure that the correct precedence and associativity are obtained in an expression.

Examples of expressions using the relational operators
If the following declarations have been made:

```
int i = 5, j= 2;
```
then the expression
```
( i - 4 ) == ( j - 1)
```
evaluates to **1** (true), and the expression
```
i < j < 3
```
is evaluated as (**i** < **j**) < 3 since the operator < (less than) has left to right associativity, the expression (**i** < **j**) evaluates to **0**, so the final comparison is (**0** < **3**) which evaluates to **1** (true).

3.1.3 The logical operators

The logical operators are[1]:

!	NOT, logical negation
&&	AND, logical and
||	OR, logical or, inclusive or

Examples of expressions using the logical operators
If the following declarations have been made

```
char c; int a, b;
```
then the expression
```
( c == 'e' )  ||  ( c == 'E' )
```
evaluates to **1** (true) when *c* is an e or E character, and the expression
```
( !a ) && ( !b )
```
evaluates to **1** when **a** is 0 and **b** is 0 (since !a and !b both have the value of 1)

Note that for both of these example expressions, the parentheses are not essential since both **&&** and || have lower precedences than the other operators.

---

[1]There are also the bitwise logical operators &, ~, ^, and |, used for low-level programming.

3.2 The selection statements: if, if else, and switch

These statements all enable a choice of actions from one or more alternatives. Each of these statements uses the value of an *expression* to determine which alternative is selected for execution. The expression must be enclosed in the parentheses (and).

In each of the following statement forms, the selected *statement-i* may be replaced by a *compound statement*.

3.2.1 The if statement has the form:

```
if ( expression ) statement-1 ;
```

The *expression* is taken to be a boolean expression:
   ◇ if the value of the expression is true (nonzero), then *statement-1* is executed,
   ◇ if the value of the expression is false (zero), *statement-1* is skipped.

3.2.2 The if else statement has the form:

```
if   ( expression )
         statement-1 ;
else     statement-2 ;
```

Again, the *expression* is taken to be a boolean expression:
   ◇ if the value of the expression is true (nonzero), then *statement-1* is executed,
   ◇ if the value of the expression is false, *statement-2* is executed.

3.2.3 Example program using the if else statement

```
/* file magic gives user one chance of guessing a magic
                                        number */
#include <iostream.h>
void main( )
{
   const int magic_number = 48;
   int guess;
   cout << "Guess the magic number! Enter a number: ";
   cin >> guess;

   if  ( guess == magic_number )
          cout << "Yes! Well done" << endl;
    else  cout << "No - try again" << endl;
}
```

We could make this program more 'user-friendly' by using another **if else** statement; this second statement is a *nested* **if else** statement. Notice how the corresponding **if** and **else** keywords are given the same amount of indentation:

```
if  ( guess == magic_number )
        cout << "Yes! Well done.";
    else    if  ( guess < magic_number )
                cout << "Too low - try higher" ;
        else    cout << "Too high - go lower";
```

3.2.4 The switch statement

The use of a **switch** statement instead of a cascade of nested **ifs** can make a program easier to read. Consider the following cascade of **ifs**, and notice how it can be replaced by **switch**, as shown in the example program in 3.2.5:

```
if ( grade == 'A' )
        cout << "Mark >= 70%";
    else    if ( grade == 'B' )
                cout << "70% > Mark >= 60%";
        else    if ( grade == 'C' )
                    cout << "60% > Mark >= 50%";
            else    if ( grade == 'D' )
                        cout << "50% > Mark >= 40%";
                else cout << "Mark < 40%";
```

The **switch** statement uses a *selector expression* that evaluates to an integer value to transfer program execution to one of a number of **cases**. A **switch** statement has the form:

```
switch  ( selector-expression )
{
   case int-val-1  :  statement-1  ;  break  ;
   case int-val-2  :  statement-2  ;  break  ;
   . . .
   case int-val-n  :  statement-n  ;  break  ;
   default :  default-statement  ;
}
```

switch compares the value of *selector-expression* to each *int-val*. If it finds a match, the corresponding statement is selected and executed. If no match is found the **default** statement is executed. **default** is optional.

The **break** statement transfers program control to *the end* of the switch statement. The use of **break** is also optional, but without it, program control passes on to the next case statement in sequence.

3.2.5 Example program showing the use of a switch statement

```
/* file grade giving the mark range corresponding to a
                                      letter grade */
#include <iostream.h>
void main( )
{
   char grade;
   cout << "Enter a grade to convert to a mark range: ";
   cin >> grade;
   switch ( grade )
     {
       case 'A' : cout << "Mark >= 70%"; break;
       case 'B' : cout << "70% > Mark >= 60%"; break;
       case 'C' : cout << "60% > Mark >= 50%"; break;
       case 'D' : cout << "50% > Mark >= 40%"; break;
       default :  cout << "Mark < 40% - a fail";
     }
}
```

In this program, any **grade** that is not one of the upper-case letters A, B, C, or D will select the **default** case.

3.3 The increment and decrement operators

These useful operators provide a 'short-hand' way of incrementing and decrementing data values. They are:

++ increment (two plus + chars)
-- decrement (two minus - chars)

Each of these operators can be used in either a *prefix* or a *postfix* form:

◇ as a *prefix operator* (e.g. ++i, --j) altering the value *before it is used*
◇ as a *postfix operator* (e.g. i++, j--) altering the value *after it has been used but before the statement is completed.*

Later example programs will use the increment and decrement operators only in simple expressions as in the following examples.

Examples of expressions using the increment and decrement operators

If the following declarations have been made:

int i = 0; char ch = 'a';

then the expression

i++

increments *i* so that its value is now 1, and the expression

++ch

increments *ch* so that it now has the value of 'b'.

3.4 The repetition statements: while, do, and for

These statements enable sequences of statements to be executed zero, once, several, or many times. Each of these statements is suitable for particular circumstances; it is important to choose which one to use carefully:

while   the sequence of statements may be executed zero or more times

do   the sequence of statements is executed at least once

for   often, but not exclusively in C++, used when the number of repetitions is known in advance.

3.4.1 The while statement

The **while** statement has the following form:

```
while  ( expression )
   statement-w ;
```

As with the **if** statements, the *expression* is taken to be a boolean expression. While the *expression* is true, *statement-w* is executed repeatedly, so *statement-w* should ensure that at some point the expression will become false. If the *expression* is false when the **while** statement is entered, *statement-w* is skipped.

3.4.2 Example program showing use of the while statement

```
/* file while counts number of e's in a sentence ending
                                  with a full-stop */
#include <iostream.h>
void main( )
{
   char c;
   int number_of_ees = 0;
   cout << "Input sentence: ";
   cin >> c;

   while ( c != '.')
   {
     if ( ( c == 'e' ) || ( c == 'E' ) )
       ++number_of_ees;
     cin >> c;
   }
   cout << "Number of E's is: " << number_of_ees << endl;
}
```

Note that if the only character input is the full-stop '.' then the compound statement within the **while** is ignored and the **number_of_ees** is output as **0**.

3.4.3 The do statement

This statement has the form:

```
do
    statement-d ;
    while ( expression ) ;
```

The **do** statement is similar to the **while** statement, except that the value of *expression* is tested after each execution of *statement-d* rather than before. So *statement-d* is executed at least once.

3.4.4 Example program showing the use of the do statement

In the following program, at least one integer is always input. If that integer is 0 then "Largest number is: 0" is written out.

```
/* file max finds the largest of an input set of
                positive integers finishing with 0 */
#include <iostream.h>
void main( )
{
   unsigned int i, max = 0;
   do
   {
      cout << "Enter a number: ";
      cin >> i;
      if ( i > max )  max = i;
   } while ( i > 0 );
   cout << "Largest number is: " << max << endl;
}
```

3.4.5 The for statement

The **for** statement is more complex than the other statements introduced in this chapter. It has the following form:

```
for ( expression-i;  expression-c;  expression-s )
    statement-f ;
```

This is equivalent to:
```
expression-i ;
while ( expression-c )
{ statement-f ;
  expression-s ;
}
```

where *expression-i* is used for initialisation and executed before any other action,

◇ *expression-c* is the control expression, repetitions will continue while it is *true*.

◇ *expression-s* may be used to step a control variable through a series of values.

3.4.6 Example program showing the use of the for statement

```
/* file for writes out a line of nine stars,
                                tab spaces apart */
#include <iostream.h>
void main( )
{
   int i;
   for ( i = 0;  i <= 8;  i++ )
      cout << '\t' << '*';
   cout << endl;
}
```

The **for** loop is equivalent to:

```
i = 0;
while  ( i <= 8 )
{
   cout << '\t' << '*';
   i++;
}
```

for statements are useful when we are handling *arrays* of *fixed numbers of data items*. The line of stars we could consider as a *one-dimensional array*.

Below is an amended version of the **main** function statements to write out a *two-dimensional array* of stars: the **for** statement, using **i** as a count, is used for the writing of the six rows, each row finishing with the use of the newline manipulator; the **for** statement, using **j** as a count, is used to the write eight tabs and spaces in each of the rows.

```
int i, j;
for ( i = 0; i <= 5; i++)
{
   for ( j = 0; j <= 8; j++ )
      cout << '\t' << '*';
   cout << endl;
}
```

3.5 The break and continue statements

We have seen the **break** statement used with a switch statement in 3.2.5. Another useful statement is the **continue** statement.

The **break** statement

```
break;
```

passes program control to just *past* the end of the nearest enclosing selection or repetition statement.

The **continue** statement

```
continue;
```

passes program control to just *before* the end of a repetition statement; it can be used only within **while, do** and **for** statements.

3.5.1 Example program showing the use of the continue statement

```
/* file continue reads in integers and finds the sum of
                                  ten non-zero ones */
#include <iostream.h>
void main( )
{
   int n, i = 0, sum = 0;
   do
    {
      cout << "Enter a number: ";
      cin >> n;
      if ( n == 0 ) continue;
        // if number is zero, go to while ( expression )
      ++i;
      sum += n;
    } while ( i < 10 );

    cout << "Sum is: " << sum << endl;
}
```

If **0** is entered, program execution passes to the control expression at the end of the **do** statement and, since **i** is unchanged, the sequence within the **do** statement is repeated.

Exercises for Chapter 3

1. Rewrite the *magic* program so that it repeats its request for input, in a user-friendly way, until the user guesses the magic number correctly.

2. Write a program to generate all the terms of the Fibonacci sequence 0, 1, 1, 2, 3, 5, 8, 13, ... less than 2000. You may assume, and start with, the initial values of 0 and 1.

3. Write a program to input a sentence ending with a full stop using the method shown in the example program in 3.4.2. Use a suitable **switch** statement to enable the counting of each of the vowels a, e, i, o, and u in the sentence, and output the number of occurrences of each vowel.

4. Write a program to count the number of words and characters in an input sentence. The sentence ends with a full stop. Assume that words are delimited by spaces, tabs, or the final full stop.
       The extraction operator does not extract 'white space' (unless a suitable manipulator is used), so to extract characters from the input stream use the **istream** *member function* **get( )** with the statement:

```
      cin.get( c );
```

This will extract one character from the input stream (which may, or may not, be a 'white space' character) and assign the character to **c**.

4 Derived types

This chapter discusses types that can be derived from the predefined types (and, as we shall see, most of them can be derived from classes as well). These types are the pointer type, the reference type, the array type, and the struct type. We consider, as well, the useful simple derived types of strings and enumerated constants.

The compiler contains the definitions of all these derived types including definitions for operators for which objects of these types may be operands.

Important operators are introduced: the reference and dereferencing operators and the selection operators.

We start with the pointer type and consider how data objects can be referred to by their addresses as well as by identifiers.

4.1 The pointer type

Pointers hold computer memory *addresses*. They are used to hide the low level details of how objects are stored in memory, but enable us to access objects, and components within these objects.

If **i** is an object of type **int** and value 65, and **p** is a pointer that holds the address of **i**, we could view them as:

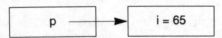

A pointer is declared with a *referenced type*. This referenced type is the type of the object whose address it normally holds.

4.1.1 Declaring and initialising pointers

Pointers are declared by placing the *dereferencing (indirection) operator* ***** between the referenced type and the pointer identifer.

These are equivalent declarations for a single pointer **p** that will hold the address of **integers**:

```
int*  p;
int   *p;
```

Both of these declaration forms are used in program examples.

If several pointers with the same referenced type are to be declared, then the dereferencing operator must be placed in front of each identifier. The following declaration, for example, declares three pointers with the **integer** reference type:

```
int *p, *q, *r;
```

Simply declaring a pointer (just requesting storage to hold an address), does not make it point to (address) anything. To use a pointer, we must initialise it to the address of an actual object using the *reference (address) operator* **&** before the identifier of the object (unless the object is an array - see 4.3).

This initialisation can be done in several ways, but the object must be declared first. For example the following sequence of statements will declare and initialise a pointer to integers:

```
int i =   65;      // declare and initialise integer i
int* p = &i;      // declare and initialise pointer p
```

4.1.2 Accessing objects using the dereferencing operator *

An object can be accessed through a pointer which holds its address using the dereferencing (indirection) operator *****.

If **p** has been declared using one of the sets of statements just given, then ***p** accesses the contents of **i**. The *dereferenced value*, ***p**, has the value of **i**. In fact, ***p** is an lvalue, and can be used as the left-hand operand of an assignment operator and with other operators that require an lvalue to be used, as the following example program shows.

i.e p may be assigned to

4.1.3 Example program showing how pointers can be used to access objects

The example program in 3.5.1 is rewritten (in a somewhat awkward way!), using a pointer **p**, which has been initialised to the address of **n** - the storage used to hold successive integers. It is dereferenced to give an lvalue, ***p**, which can be used as an alternative to the identifier **n**.

```
/* file pointer reads in integers and finds the sum of
                            ten non-zero ones */
#include <iostream.h>
void main( )
{                              * p is n contents
   int n, i = 0, sum = 0;
   int* p = &n;
               // declaring and initialising pointer p
   do
   {
      cout << "Enter number: ";
      cin >> *p;  // using *p to store the value of n
      if ( n == 0 )              // using the identifier n
         continue;
      ++i;
      sum += *p;
                  //  the value of *p is the value of n
   } while ( i < 10 );

   cout << "Sum is: " << sum << endl;
}
```

4.1.3 Operators used with pointers

The increment and decrement operators are frequently used with pointers. *When a pointer is incremented, it is incremented by the size of the storage required by an object of the referenced type.* When a pointer is decremented, it is decremented by the size of the storage required by an object of the referenced type.

Other operators that we will use with pointers include the *assignment* operator and the *indirect selection* operator (introduced in 4.7.2). In a later chapter, the *type cast* operator will be used to change the referenced type of a pointer.

Pointers will be used frequently throughout the rest of this book. In particular, they are closely associated with *arrays* in C and C++, and they provide the easiest way of accessing characters in a string. But they will also allow us to access members of *structs* (later in this chapter) and members of *classes* (in later chapters).

4.2 Reference types

A reference type can be used to declare a *reference* - a new, alternative, name for an object of a given type. A reference is an 'alias' for an identifier.

C programmers should note that these types are not defined in C. The use of reference types enables passing arguments to functions by reference, and a reference type can be used as the return type of a function (see Chapter 5).

4.2.1 Declaring references

A reference can be initialised to an lvalue when it is declared, and thereafter can be used as an alternative name for the object. If it is initialised with a value that is not an lvalue, then a new object is created to hold that value.

References are declared by placing the *reference operator* **&** between the type and the reference identifier. For example, if the declaration **int i;** has been made, then we can declare and initialise the reference **j** by using the declaration:

```
int&  j = i;
```

After this statement, **j** is also now an identifier for the value of **i**.

It should be noted that if a reference is used on the left-hand side of an assignment statement to alter the contents of an object, then the alteration of the contents will apply for any other identifiers of that object as well.

4.2.2 Example program showing the use of a reference

This example program is yet another version of that first shown in 3.5.1. This time a reference is declared as an alternative name for the object that holds the integers in turn.

```
/* file reference reads in integers and finds the sum of
                              ten non-zero ones */
#include <iostream.h>
void main( )
{
    int n, i = 0, sum = 0;
    int& m = n;
                   // declaring and initialising reference m
    do
    {
        cout << "Enter number: ";
        cin >> m;          // using alternative name for n
        if ( n == 0 )      // using original identifier n
            continue;
        ++i;
        sum += m;          // using alternative name for n
    } while ( i < 10 );
    cout << "Sum is: " << sum << endl;
}
```

4.3 Arrays

An array is the simplest data object in C++ that can hold more than one value: an *array* contains a fixed number of data object components, *all of the same type* that can be selected by *position*.

The values stored in an array are the *components* (elements) of the array. The *type of the component objects* is the *type of the array*. The numbers that indicate the positions of the components are *subscripts* (indices): their type is the *subscript type* (or index type). The components of an array may be of any type; the subscript type, however, must be an integer type. Array components are always subscripted (indexed) *starting from zero*. Subscripts are non-negative integers.

4.3.1 One-dimensional arrays and the subscript operator

The components of a one-dimensional array are stored one after another in a single 'row' or 'column'. To declare an array, we must specify the type of an array's components, and the number of components.

Example of a one dimensional-array
Suppose the following ten integer values are to be stored in an array:

3	–5	7	99	1	6	–46	17	9	74

The array could be declared by the statement:

```
int a[ 10 ];
```

which declares an array whose identifier is **a** with ten components of type **int**.

If the integers are read into the array in the order given above, then

```
a[ 0 ]   // a[ 0 ] is an lvalue with contents of  3
a[ 1 ]   // a[ 1 ] is an lvalue with contents of -5
. .
a[ 9 ]   // a[ 9 ] is an lvalue with contents of 74
```

The subscript operator **[ ]** is used in the declaration to hold the number of components of the array.

An lvalue (identifier) for the second component (say) is obtained by using the array identifier with **1** enclosed within the subscript operator, so in this array it is given by **a[1]**.

Since the components of this array are all integers, we can use the integer operators to handle them in expression statements and expressions such as:

```
a[ 4 ]  =  -13;
```

which assigns a new value to the fifth component, and

```
k = a[ 6 ]  +  a[ 7 ];
```

where components are added and the result assigned, and

```
if  ( a[ 8 ]  >  a[ 9 ] ) . .
```

where the relational operators can be used to compare components.

4.3.2 Example program showing array declaration and handling

The **for** statement is particularly useful for accessing the contents of each component of an array in turn.

```
/* file reverse reads ten integers into an array and
               then writes them out in reverse order */
#include <iostream.h>
#define N 10          // macro definition, 10 replaces N
void main( )
{
   int a[ N ],  i;
            // declaring an integer array and an integer
   cout << "Enter ten numbers: ";
   for ( i = 0 ; i < N ; i++ )
     cin >> a[ i ];     // reading in an array component
   cout << "In reverse order: ";
   for ( i = N - 1 ; i >= 0 ; i-- )
     cout << a[ i ] << " ";
          // writing the value of a component and a space
}
```

This program also uses the **define** *directive* to the preprocessor of the compiler. **define** defines a *macro*: the preprocessor replaces the word immediately following the directive by the second word, wherever it occurs in the program, before the program is compiled.

The ability to write such macro[1] definitions is inherited from the C language, but these definitions can lead to ambiguities and they are not often used now within C++ program code.

4.3.3 Initialising one-dimensional arrays

An array may be given a set of initial values by using an *array initialiser* (a list of constant expressions enclosed in braces) when it is declared. If the initialiser is *shorter* than the array, the remaining components of the array are given the value of 0. If an initialiser is present, the length of the array may be omitted.

Examples of integer array declarations using array initialisers
```
    int a[ 5 ] = { 2,  4,  6,  8,  10 };
```
where initialiser gives all the values of **a**, and
```
    int b[ 5 ] = { 1,  3,  5 };
```
where the initial values of **b** are 1, 3, 5, 0, 0, and
```
    int c[ ]   = { 7,  9 };
```
where the array **c** has, implicitly, two components.

4.3.4 An array identifier is a constant pointer

The name of an array is a constant pointer to the first component of the array. The identifier of an array holds the address of the first component, and this address cannot be changed.

Because the array identifier is a constant pointer, it cannot be used to step through the components of the array, so its value is often first assigned to a non-constant pointer with the same referenced type.

This second pointer may be incremented (or decremented) so that it then holds the address of the succeeding (or preceding) array component.

4.3.5 Example program using a pointer to access array components

The previous example program is rewritten using pointers. The identifier **a** of the array is a constant pointer whose value is an address that cannot be changed (the address of **a[0]**).

A non-constant pointer **p** with the **int** referenced type is declared. In the first **for** statement, **p** is initially assigned the address of the first component, dereferenced to read in the value of that component, and then incremented until it holds the address, **&a[N - 1]**, of the last component of the array.

---

[1]Macro definitions are frequently found within library modules, since they can be used to replace general identifiers with implementation-specific values, e.g. MAX_INT.

To write them out in reverse order, in the second **for** statement **p** is first assigned the address of the last component and decremented until it holds the address of the first component, **a**.

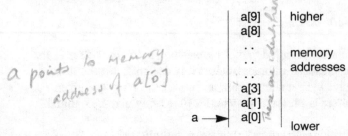

```
                        a[9]    higher
                        a[8]
                         . .    memory
                         . .    addresses
                         . .
                        a[3]
                        a[1]
                a ──▶   a[0]
                                lower
```

a points to memory address of a[0]

Above is a diagram showing how the components of the array are stored in memory, **p** can point to (hold the address of) any component of **a**

```
/* file array reads ten integers into an array and
                    then writes them in reverse order */
#include <iostream.h>
#define N 10

void main( )
{
   int a[ N ], *p;
   cout << "Enter ten integers: ";

   for ( p = a ; p <= &a[ N - 1 ] ; p++ )
     cin >> *p;

   cout << "In reverse order: ";

   for ( p = &a[ N - 1 ] ; p >= a ; p-- )
     cout << *p << " ";
}
```

sets up the addresses

p = address of 1st element of array

into machine now placed 1st content now put equal to element 1st element number

4.3.5 Multi-dimensional arrays

An array may have any number of dimensions. In declarations, the number of components in each dimension is enclosed by the subscript operator [ ]. A declaration of a two-dimensional integer array with three 'rows' and three 'columns' might be:

        int   r[3] [3];

The subscripts of each dimension start with 0, so the element of **r** in the second row, third column can be accessed using the lvalue **r[1] [2]**.

An initialiser for a two-dimensional array can be created by nesting one-dimensional initialisers. A declaration and initialisation of a two-dimensional array could be:

        int I[3][3] = {{1, 0, 0},{0, 1, 0},{0, 0, 1}} ;

4.4 Strings

A *string* is a one-dimensional array of **chars** ending with the null character, '\0', as the string terminator.

4.4.1 String literals

A *string literal* is a sequence of characters enclosed by double quotes as in
```
"Hello world!\n"
```
We have already used them many times in **cout** statements, sometimes including escape sequences.

String literals may be continued over more than one line. When two or more string literals are adjacent (separated only by white space) the compiler is required to join them into a single string as in:
```
cout <<   "This is one string "  "and a second string"
      " and a third string that will be joined onto it\n";
```
The compiler places a *null* character terminator '\0' at the end of each string literal, so a string literal of **n chars** actually occupies **n + 1 chars** of memory.

A string literal is represented by a constant pointer to its first character, since it is an array. It can be used to initialise a string where the length of the char array does not need to be given; for example:
```
char hangman[ ] = "HANGMAN";
```
declares and initialises a char array of 8 components including the null terminator.

4.4.2 String objects

A *string* is just a one-dimensional array of **char**acters, but remember, when declaring an array of chars that will be used to hold a string, *always to make the array one character longer than the string* because of the null terminator. Removing the null character, or failing to leave room for it, can cause unpredictable results when a program is executed, since all functions in the ANSI C libraries assume that strings are null terminated, as we will see in the example in 4.6. (We will later see how to define a string class where strings are not necessarily terminated by the null character.)

4.4.5 Example program showing the declaration and searching of a string

This is a reworking of the example program 3.4.2 which counted the number of e's in a sentence, this time counting the number of e's in a word.

The word is read in from **cin** using the extraction operator. The extraction operator can be used to read in a string, but it terminates reading when it meets 'white space', so we can only use it to read in a single word. The string extraction operation places a null terminator '\0' at the end of the string read in.

The insertion operator can be used to output a string when required.

The string is read into the array **word[20]**, where **word** is a constant pointer to the first letter in the string. A pointer **p**, of referenced type **char**, is declared which holds the addresses of successive letters in the string.

```
// file ees counts the number of e's in a word string
#include <iostream.h>

void main( )
{
    char word[ 20 ], *p;
            // declaration of a string and a char pointer
    int number_of_ees = 0;

    cout << "Input word: ";
    cin >> word;
        // reading string, extraction stops at white space
    for ( p = word ; *p != '\0'; p++ )
        if ( ( *p == 'e' ) || ( *p == 'E' ) )
            ++number_of_ees;
    cout << "The number of e's in your word is: "
            << number_of_ees << endl ;
}
```

At the beginning of the **for** loop, **p** is assigned the address of the first letter in the word. The char at this location is examined to see if it is an upper or lower case **e**, and the count increased if it is an **e** or an **E**.

p is then incremented to point to the next character, and the next character is examined to see if it is the null terminator. If it is, then the **for** loop terminates.

4.5 Using the string library

The C++ language provides little support for strings: they are treated as arrays, and restricted in the same way as arrays. In particular, *they cannot be assigned or compared.*

We can use functions from the ANSI C **string** library instead, to handle strings. Programs that use functions from this library should contain the directive:

```
#include <string.h>
```

The functions whose prototypes are given in **string.h** have arguments of type **char***, so arguments can be a pointer with the char referenced type, or the identifier of a string, or the identifier of a string literal. (Functions are discussed in more detail in the next chapter.)

Appendix 6 gives declarations and full comments for most of the functions to be found in this library. Some of the most useful are briefly introduced here:

```
strcpy( s1, s2 )
```
copies string s2 into string s1; and

```
strcat( s1,   s2 )
```
appends s2 to the end of s1; and

```
     strcmp ( s1, s2 )
```
compares s1 to s2, returning an integer value; and
```
     strlen ( s )
```
returns the number of chars in s up to, but not including, the first null char.

4.5.2 Example program using string.h functions giving a run-time error

The following simple program illustrates the use of functions from the **string** library. If it is only 'played' once, then no problems arise, but playing more than once shows how unpredictable results can occur when strings are not handled carefully! A typical execution of the program using Turbo C++ produced:

```
Enter a word: sheep
Your word is: sheep
The length of your word is: 5
Enter a second word: goat
You have given different words
Play with strings? Answer y/n: y
heep
```

The string "**Enter a word**" has been overwritten by part of the first word!

```
// file playstr playing with string functions
#include <iostream.h>
#include <string.h>                  // using string library
void main ( )
{
   char enter_message [ ] = "Enter a word: ";
   char response [ ] = "\nYour word is: ";
                        // string literal declarations
   char word1 [20], word2 [20], ch;
   do
     {
       cout << enter_message;
       cin >> word1;                          // read word1
       cout << strcat ( response, word1 ) << endl;
               // add word1 to end of response and write
       cout << "\nThe length of your word is: "
            << strlen ( word1 );
       cout << "\n\nEnter a second word: ";
       cin >> word2;                          // read word2
       char word3 [20];                  // declare word3
       strcpy ( word3 , word2 );      // initialise word3
       if ( strcmp (word1 , word3) == 0 ) // compare words
            cout << "\nYour words are both the same\n";
       else cout << "\nYou have given different words\n";
       cout << "Play with strings? Answer y/n: " ;
       cin  >> ch;
     } while ( ch != 'n' )
}
```

The error is caused by appending the first word entered, **word1**, to **response** without considering how these strings are stored in memory.

Obviously there was no storage available in **response** for **word1**.

But in considering why **word1** overran **enter_message** we can begin to consider more general points concerned with storage.

Data objects declared in a block are *local* to that block, and are normally stored on the program's run-time *stack*. This stack is a *last-in-first-out* (LIFO) *store which usually increases downwards* through memory.

Within a block, data objects are stored on the stack, in decreasing address locations, in the order in which they are declared. But within an array, *the components are usually stored in upwards memory order*. So the strings were stored, using Turbo C++, as shown in this diagram:

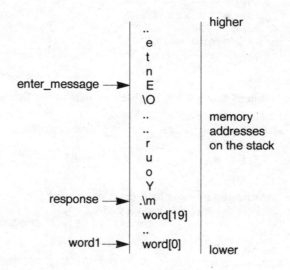

So if **word1** is "sheep", say, which is concatenated onto the end of **response**, the use of **strcat(response, word1)** causes 's' to overwrite the null terminator of the string **response** and then the characters 'h' 'e' 'e' 'p' and '\0' overwrite 'E' 'n' 't' 'e' and 'r' in **enter_message**.

The statement

```
    cout << enter_message;
```

writes the string pointed to by **enter_message** which now holds the address of 'h', and so **cout** extracts the string finishing at the null terminator after 'p'.

In Chapter 8 a similar program is shown where such an error does not occur. A mystring class is defined so that a string object of this class cannot be appended onto another if there is insufficient storage space to hold it. This new string class is much closer to string types found in the libraries of languages which are strongly typed and which do not allow such run-time errors to occur.

4.6 Enumerated constants

This is a simple derived type where a user may define a list of *identifiers* each associated with an **int**eger object. If we do not specify otherwise, enumerated constants identify positive integer values starting from zero.

Example declarations of enumerated constants
```
       enum weekday { MON, TUE, WED, THURS, FRI };
```
where the enumeration list identifier is **weekday** and the enumerated constants are **MON** with a value of 0, **TUE** with a value of 1, etc.
```
       enum days { MON=3, TUE=6, WED=2, THURS=9, FRI=5 };
```
for these enumerated constants, **MON** has a value of 3, **TUE** a value of 6, etc.

The most useful application for enumerations is to implement boolean values with the declaration:
```
       enum boolean { FALSE, TRUE };
```
where **FALSE** is the identifier of an object with an integer value of **0** and **TRUE** is the identifier of an object with the value of **1**. This declaration will be used frequently in later example programs.

4.7 Structs and the selection operators

A **struct**ure is a definition of a related collection of *data members*. These data members can be of any type. A structure is similar to a *record* with *fields*, a type found in other languages.

As we shall see, a **struct** is a very simple form of a class. They are discussed here mainly to introduce two selection operators that will be used extensively in later chapters.

A struct is defined using the keyword **struct** followed by the *struct_identifier*, the list of data members is enclosed by braces and the definition finishes with a semi-colon ;.

In the following example program, in 4.7.3, a **struct** *record* with members *name* and *id* is defined as:

```
struct record
{
    char name[ MAX_WORD + 1 ];      // data member name
    int id;                         // data member id
};                   // note semi-colon after closing brace
```

After a struct, *struct_identifier*, has been defined, objects of type *struct_identifier* can be declared, and pointers with *struct_identifier* as the referenced type can also be declared.

When a *struct_identifier* object has been declared, storage space for each of the data members is allocated in succesive locations in memory.

In the following example program, an array with identifier **group** whose components are three objects with type **record** is declared with the statement:

```
record group[ MAX_RECORDS ];
```

A pointer with the *record* referenced type is declared with the statement:

```
record* p;
```

There are two operators that can be used to access the members of a struct object: the direct selection operator . (the 'dot' operator), and the indirect selection operator ->.

4.7.1 The direct selection operator

The direct selection operator has two operands: the left operand is the *object_identifier* and the right operand is the *member_identifier* selected.

This operator is used twice in the example program where the record details are entered; it is used in the expression

```
group[ i ] . name
```

and in the expression

```
group[ i ] . id
```

4.7.2 The indirect selection operator

The indirect selection operator is also a binary operator, but *the left operand is a pointer* with the referenced type of *struct_identifier* and the right operand is the *member_identifier* selected.

We have seen that an array identifier is a constant pointer to the first component of an array. If the array has components of type *struct_identifier* we can initialise a pointer to *struct_identifier*s to the address of the first component, and then make it point later to any of the components of the array as required.

In the example program, this initialisation can be seen in the first control expression of the second **for** statement, in

```
p = group
```

The members of each record are then indirectly selected in turn, within the **for** statement, in the expression

```
p -> name
```

and in the expression

```
p -> id
```

The pointer **p** is incremented and used in a similar way to the pointer used to step through an array as discussed in 4.3.4.

Note that the members could have been accessed using the dereferencing operator * and the direct selector operator ., as in **(*p).name**. Using the indirect selection operator is equivalent to using these two operators in such an expression.

4.7.3 Example program showing how members of a struct can be accessed

The program inputs the name and identification number of a group of three people and then outputs these details. Notice that **MAX_NAME** and **MAX_RECORDS** are defined and declared as constant objects; alternatively they could have been given macro definitions here.

```
/* file structs accessing members with the selection
                                         operators */
#include <iostream.h>

const MAX_NAME = 20;
const MAX_RECORDS = 3;

void main( )
{
  struct record          //  definition of struct record
    {
      char name[ MAX_NAME + 1 ];     // data member name
      int id;                        // data member id
    };

  record group[ MAX_RECORDS ];
          // declaring an array of three record objects
  record* p;              // declaring a pointer to records

  cout << "enter records" << endl;
      // entering member values using direct selection
  for ( int i = 0; i < MAX_RECORDS; i++ )
    {
      cout << "enter name: ";
      cin >> group[ i ] . name;
      cout << "enter id: ";
      cin >> group[ i ] . id;
    }

  cout << "your records are: " << endl;
      // writing member values using indirect selection
  for ( p = group; p < &group[ MAX_RECORDS ]; p++ )
    {
      cout << "name: " << p -> name << endl;
      cout << "id: " << p -> id << endl;
    }
}
```

In this program, **i** has been declared when it is needed - in the initialisation expression of the first **for** statement.

This example program also demonstrates that it is permissible to compare the address in a pointer with the address of an undeclared object **group[MAX_RECORDS]** (group[3]), but the contents of this undeclared location should not be accessed.

Exercises for Chapter 4

1. The first innings scores of the England Team in a recent Test Match with India were:

   17, 0, 33, 1, 1, 17, 28, 21, 4, 17, 4 (India won the match by eight wickets).

Read these scores into an array, and then display them showing, for each score, how much each score differed from the average score for the team.

2. Draw a 'horizontal' histogram for the Test innings scores given in the first question, as in:

   17 *****************
   0
   33 *******************************
   ...

3. A palindrome is a word that reads the same forwards and backwards, like *madam* and *radar*. Read in words of up to 20 letters, and test each one to see if it is a palindrome.

4. When the extraction operator >> is used to read, a predefined data object is read in until a *white space* character (space, tab, newline) is encountered.

   cin is a data object (*instance*) of the **istream** class. We can use the member function **getline( )** of this class to read in a string *s* (that may include spaces and tabs) until either a specified *count* of input characters is reached or a *newline* char is encountered, as in

```
        cin.getline( s, count, '\n' );.
```
We use the *dot operator* between the class object and the class member function that handles such an object. (*count* is usually the maximum line length or less.)

   Read in a line using this function and count the numbers of vowels occurring in that line. Vowels are the characters 'a', 'e', 'i', 'o', and 'u'.

5. A bookshop manager keeps details of the Author, Title, Publisher, and Price for each of the books in stock in a shop.

   Write a program that will input the details of four books and then enable the manager to output the other details of one of these books whose title has been requested by a customer.

6. Write a program that can adjust the length of lines. The program should read in a long line, request a short line length and then output the long line in several lines of short line length.

   Rewrite the program so that the short lines are both left and right justified within the short line length. [Difficult!]

5 Functions

One of the most fundamental ideas in problem solving, and for developing an *algorithm* to obtain a solution, is to divide a problem into smaller subproblems each independent of other subproblems, solve each of the subproblems and hence solve the original problem.

This chapter looks at *functions*, where a *function* is a subprogram used to solve a particular task within a program. Each function solves a subproblem of the original programming task. Functions are small program sections.

The **main( )** function of a program ensures that the overall task of a program is carried out. Other functions can be *called* for use by the **main( )** function, and by further functions.

Functions may have *argument* (parameter) values passed to them, and may **return** values. Functions are similar to the procedures or subroutines of other languages. It should be noted that C++ functions cannot be nested.

This chapter also introduces the terms *scope* and *duration*.

5.1 Function definition, declaration and call

The words *definition* and *declaration* have specific meanings when used with C++ functions.

A *function definition* is the place where the full form of the function is stored. It is usually placed after the **main( )** function, or with the function declaration (if it is an **inline** function), or in a library. This chapter shows how definitions are placed within a program. Chapter 6 shows how function definitions can be given in a library.

A *function declaration* (also known as a function *prototype*) gives to the compiler the identifier of the function and the types of the argument and a return-type, so that it can associate the correct definition with the function_identifier when it is used subsequently in a function call. A function declaration must be made before a function definition can be used; it is usually placed before the **main( )** function.

5.1.1 A function definition

The general form of a function definition is:

```
return_type function_identifier ( formal_arguments )
{
    statements;
    return_statement;
                // need not be used if return_type is void
}
```

The *return_type* of a function is the type of the object that the function **return**s. Functions may not return *arrays*, but there is no other restriction on the return_type. If the return_type is omitted, the function is assumed to return a value of type **int**[1]. If a return_type is **void**, the function does not return anything.

After the function_identifier comes a parenthesised list of *formal_arguments*. Each formal argument is preceded by its type. Formal arguments are separated by commas in the list. If the function has no arguments, the word **void** can appear between the parentheses (and).

An identifier is shown to be a *function_identifier* by including parentheses after the identifier.

The portion of a function definition between **{** and **}** is the *body* of the function, and may contain declaration and executable statements, as in the **main( )** function.

5.1.2 A function declaration, also known as a function prototype

The general form of a function declaration is:

```
return_type function_identifier ( formal_arguments ) ;
```

A function declaration is usually the same as the *header line* of a function definition, but finished with a *semi-colon* **;**. (We shall see a modification when we consider class member functions.)

A function must be declared before it is used.

The formal arguments may just be given by type in the declaration (prototype).

5.1.3 Function calls (except in-line function calls)

A function is *called* (used, executed) by using its *function_identifier* in a statement, together with the *actual arguments* (the actual objects) that we want the function to use at that point.

When program control passes from one function to another, the system must remember the point in the calling function to which it must return. A *stack-frame* is set up, on a function call, on the *program run-time stack*, and the *return address* is stored in the frame. Data objects that are declared in the called function are also given storage space in the stack-frame. The actual arguments are also passed to the called function on the frame: either a *copy* of the value of the argument (for an argument *passed by value*), or the *address* of the argument (for an argument *passed by reference*).

---

[1]When C++ programs are entered on the Unix operating system, often no return-type is apparently given to the **main( )** function. In fact, the return-type is then implicitly **int**.

When the called function has completed executing, the return address is obtained from the stack-frame, *and the stack-frame is then cleared*. This means that the data objects declared by the second function also disappear: they exist only while the called function is executing.

5.1.4 Example program showing a simple function and type conversions

This program inputs a decimal monetary value (in pounds, dollars, etc.) and, after performing some arithmetic calculations, uses the function *round( )* to output another monetary value with two fractional places (the pence, cents, etc.).

The function *round( )* is used instead of the manipulator **setprecision(2)**.

```
// file vat adds the Value Added Tax to an original cost
#include <iostream.h>
double round( double );          // function declaration
void main( )
{
   const double vatpercent = 17.5;
   double cost, vat;
   cout << "Input original cost: ";
   cin >> cost;
   vat = cost * vatpercent / 100.0;
   cost += vat;
   cost = round( cost );
              // function call, cost is actual argument
   cout << "Cost including VAT is " << cost;
}
/* function definition of a function that rounds off a
double to two decimal places, x is a formal argument */
double round( double x )
{
   long y = long(100.0 * x + 0.5);
                // change to integer to impose accuracy
   return ( double(y) / 100.0 );
                              // return a double value
}
```

The effect of the function **round( )** can be seen if we work through the program with an original (pretax) cost where **cost** is input with a value of **12.50**.

vat is calculated using **vat = 12.50 * 17.5 / 100.0**, giving **vat = 2.1875**. The new **cost**, including the vat tax, is then **12.50 + 2.1875** which is **14.6875**. But we want to output a monetary cost correct to two decimal places (giving the pence, cents, etc.). So this new **cost** is made the actual argument of the function **round( )**. It replaces the formal argument x of this function.

Within the function, an integer **long** is declared, with an identifier of y, and initialised with the value **long(100.0 * 14.6875 + 0.5)**. The arithmetic expression in the parentheses evaluates to **1469.25**. This is now converted to a **long** integer value, so that the value of y is **1469** (losing the fractional part).

Finally, the return_value of the function is evaluated: **double(1469) / 100.0**. The type conversion gives the division: **1469.00 / 100.0**. So the value returned is **14.69**.

This is then assigned to **cost**, in the statement **cost = round( )**, so that it can be output as required.

5.2 Passing arguments by value and by reference

The *formal_argument list* within a function declaration, and a function definition header line, may be referred to as the *signature* of the function. C++ is, in many respects, a *strongly-typed* language, and the types of the actual arguments in a function call are checked by the compiler to see that they agree with the corresponding types of the formal arguments that they are replacing. Moreover, as we will see in Chapter 8, a function identifier can be associated with several definitions (overloading). The compiler uses the signature (the types of the arguments) to determine which definition to bind to the code when a function identifier is used in a function call.

Within the argument list, the arguments are given by their type (passing by value) or by their reference type (passing by reference). The components of the list are separated by commas. If there are no arguments to be passed, the parentheses ( ) are left empty or contain the word **void**.

5.2.1 Passing arguments by value

This method causes *a copy of the value* of the actual argument to be passed into the formal argument of the function. The *copy* of the data object is used by the function, and altered as necessary. *The data item in the calling block is left untouched*. This method should be used whenever possible, since it produces no changes in the calling function.

Arguments passed by value are given in the *formal_argument* list of the function declaration and definition header line by their *type* and by the *identifier* of the argument used within the function definition. The *identifier* may be omitted from the formal_argument list given in the function declaration (prototype).

5.2.2 Passing arguments by reference

This method passes *the address* of the actual argument to the function. This means that changes made to the argument data object inside the function *are known to the calling function*.

The types of the arguments passed by reference in the formal argument list are either a *reference type* (*type&*) or a pointer *referenced type* (*type**).

Arrays are always passed by reference to functions since an array identifier is a constant pointer whose referenced type is the type of its components. To prevent changes being made to the components of an array, the array can be made a **const**ant object. A constant object pointer can then be used within a function to examine, but not modify, the components (see 5.6.4).

5.2.3 *Example program showing the two methods of passing arguments*

When this program is executed, the successive outputs from the **main( )** function show how the integer input has been handled by the function *value_arg( )* (to which it is passed by value), and the function *reference_arg()* (to which it is passed by reference). The first function leaves the value of the integer in the **main( )** function unchanged; the second function alters it. An execution run gave:

```
Enter an integer: 3
Integer after being used as a value argument is 3
Integer after being used as a reference argument is 15
```

```
// file argument1
#include <iostream.h>

void value_arg( int );
    // function declaration, argument passed by value
void ref_arg( int& );
    // function declaration, argument passed by reference
void main( )
{
  int i;
  cout << "Enter an integer: ";
  cin >> i;
  value_arg( i );                      /* function call,
            i is actual argument passed by value */
  cout << "Integer after being used"
          " as a value argument is " << i << endl;
  ref_arg( i );                        /* function call,
          i is actual argument passed by reference */
  cout << "Integer after being used"
          " as a reference argument is " << i << endl;
}

// function definition, h is a formal argument
void value_arg( int h )
{ h *= 4;  }       // function multiplies argument by 4

// function definition, k is a formal argument
void ref_arg( int& k )
{ k *= 5;  }       // function multiplies argument by 5
```
Note that the formal argument identifiers need not be given in a function declaration.

5.3 Return values and the return statement

The alternative method of passing a value back to the calling function is to use one or more statements of the form

```
return object_of_return_type ;
```

The type of the returned object must be the same as the return_type.

When a **return** statement is executed, the function in which it is encountered is terminated and program control is passed back to the calling block. It is possible to have more than one **return** statement written into a function, but only one will be executed. The *value of the object_of_return_type* is also passed back. The value may be used in an expression (including an assignment expression statement) in the block that called the function. Again, a C++ compiler will check that the types of the values agree.

5.4 Inline functions

Sometimes, as in the previous example program, function definitions are so short that the overhead associated with a normal function call seriously increases the execution time (setting up the stack-frame, storing values on it, clearing the stack frame). In C++ we have an alternative function implementation: *inline functions*. Here, every time a function call is encountered, the compiler replaces the function identifier with the full function definition. This increases the speed of execution, but also increases the length of the program code, so inline functions are usually as small as possible.

The declaration and definition of an inline function are given together; the declaration is usually preceded by the keyword **inline**.

5.4.1 Rewriting the previous example program using inline functions

```
// file argument2
#include <iostream.h>
inline void value_arg( int h )  {  h *= 4;  }
inline void ref_arg( int& k)   {  k *= 5;  }
void main( )
{ int i;
  cout << "Enter an integer: ";
  cin >> i;
  value_arg( i );
  cout << "Integer after being used"
              " as a value argument is " << i << endl;
  ref_arg( i );
  cout << "Integer after being used"
              " as a reference argument is " << i << endl;
}
```

This version, with two inline function definitions and declarations, gives the same response to the input integer as the program in 5.2.3.

5.5 The comma operator

The comma operator can be used to form one expression from two or more expressions. For example, if **i** and **j** have both been declared integers, the single expression statement

```
i = 3, j = 5;
```

performs both of the assignments within one statement.

This operator has the lowest precedence of all the operators and so can be used to combine any expressions formed using other operators. It is commonly used in **for** statements, as in the next example program.

5.6 The first version of a program that plays the hangman game

To illustrate how functions can be used to solve non-trivial tasks, we consider a first approach to writing a program that allows the user to play a game of hangman. In the next chapter we will consider how to improve this version.

Here we develop a program that, after asking the user to input a word (!), asks the user to guess the letters in the word. If a wrong guess is made the word HANGMAN is gradually built up on the screen. The user can carry on playing until she/he requests otherwise.

A typical execution run might be:

```
Word please: zoo
Mask is             ---
Letter please: a
You are hanging the man . . .   H
Mask is             ---
Letter please: e
You are hanging the man . . .   HA
Mask is             ---
Letter please: o
Good.
Mask is             -oo
Letter please: z
Good.
Mask is             zoo
Well done! You found the word!
Play? Answer yes/no: no
```

5.6.1 The hangman data objects

The data objects that need to be manipulated in this program module are *word*, *mask*, and the input *letter*. In this first approach, we will manipulate these data objects with general functions in the program. In subsequent chapters we will associate data objects much more closely with the specific functions that manipulate them.

5.6.2 Developing a hangman program using functional decomposition

In this first approach we write an outline of the **main( )** function, sketching in other functions for small, detailed, tasks and using structure statements to ensure that program control will proceed in an ordered way. This is *functional decomposition*.

Here we are solving a non-trivial problem using *the principle of abstraction* in a *top-down design*. The term *abstraction* is used when the solution of a task is considered without all the details of the realisation.

The basic idea behind *abstracting top-down design*, which goes back to Dijkstra (1969) and Wirth (1971), is that the act of design should start with the analysis of the system specification and should ignore the details of the implementation. A task is decomposed, topdown, into subtasks until functions are available which are easily formulated.

Only when an overview is obtained of the complete solution should the solution be written in detail.

5.6.3 A functional decomposition of the hangman task

The functions that will implement the subtasks are shown in italics:

```
do
{    cout << "Word please: ";  cin >> word;
     initial_mask( );
     print_mask( );
     do
     { letter = get_letter( );
       if ( letter_in_word( ) )
              update_mask( );
       else    print_hangman( );
       print_mask( );
     } while ( ( !hangman_complete( ) ) && ( !letters_all_found( ) ) );

     if ( hangman_complete( ) ) cout << "\n\nI won - you lost!";
     else cout << "\n\nWell done! You found the word!";

     cout << "Play? Answer yes/no: ";  cin >> reply;
} while ( reply == yes );
```

5.6.4 Implementing the functions

Since we are dealing with words as strings, we will need to know their maximum length, and we will need to have the length of lines to recognise when the end of a line is reached. Constants can be declared for these together with a 'user-friendly' identifier, **EOS,** for the string null terminator.

Several of the functions are used in boolean expressions where a *false* or *true* value must be returned. The enumerated constants definition and declaration
enum boolean { FALSE, TRUE };
can be made before function declarations so that the compiler has knowledge of **TRUE** and **FALSE** before they are used in any function definitions.

A few of the functions defined in the program are discussed here. New input and output features used in other functions are discussed after the program code in 5.6.6.

The function *initial_mask( )* should make **mask** contain the same number of '-' (hyphen) characters as there are characters in the input **word** string. It will have a return type of **void** since it does not return a value. It needs to have two formal arguments: a constant argument s1 for the **word** that should not be altered by the function, and an argument s2 for the corresponding **mask** that will be formed by the function.

String identifiers are constant pointers that cannot be changed, so we need to declare, within the function, pointers that are initialised to the start of the strings and can then be incremented to point to each of the characters in the strings in turn. Note that the **const**ant argument **s1** requires a corresponding **const**ant referenced type for this pointer.

A **for** statement can be used to step through the two strings. It will not need an initialisation expression since the pointer used in the control expression is already declared and initialised. Both of the pointers can be incremented using the comma operator within the final step expression.

So the function can be written as:

```
void initial_mask( const char* s1, char* s2 )
{
    const char* p = s1;
    // p points to constant chars that cannot be altered

    char* q = s2;
        // q points to chars in s2 that will be altered

    for ( ; *p != EOS ; p++, q++ )
        *q = '-';
            // hyphens in mask correspond to chars in word

    *q = EOS;
            // mask string finished with null terminator
}
```

The functions *letter_in_word( )* and *letters_all_found( )* both need to return a boolean value. Again, a **for** statement can be used in each function to step through the strings. In both cases, if a certain condition is found to be true while stepping through the strings, a **return** statement returning TRUE can be used to exit from the function at that point; if the condition is not found, then a final **return** statement returning FALSE will be reached.

5.6.5 The first version of the hangman program: game1

```
// file game1
#include <iostream.h>

const EOS = '\0';
const MAX_WORD = 20;
const LINE_LENGTH = 80;

enum boolean { FALSE, TRUE };

// function declarations
char get_letter( );
            // returns a letter input from the keyboard
void initial_mask( const char* , char* );
        /* constructs a mask for a word to be guessed,
                        arguments are word and mask */
void print_mask( const char* );
    // writes current state of mask, argument is mask
int letter_in_word( const char*, char );
        /* returns TRUE if a guessed letter is in a word
                            else returns FALSE,
                    arguments are word and letter */
void update_mask( const char*, char*, char );
        /* places correctly guessed letter of word into
                    corresponding positions of mask,
                arguments are word, mask, and letter */
void print_hangman( int );
        // argument is count of wrongly guessed letters
inline int hangman_complete( int count )
{ return ( count == 7 ); }
                // returns TRUE if HANGMAN fully written
int letters_all_found( const char* );
        /* returns TRUE if all the letters in a mask
                    are found else returns FALSE,
                        argument is mask */
// main function definition
void main( )
{
    char word[ MAX_WORD + 1 ], mask[ MAX_WORD + 1 ];
    char letter, reply;
    do                      // do for each play of the game
    {
        cout << "Word please: ";          // request new word
        cin >> word;                     // read word to guess
        cin.ignore( LINE_LENGTH, '\n' );
                                    // ignore rest of line
        int count = 0;      /* declare and initialise count
                            of wrongly guessed letters */
        initial_mask( word, mask );   // make mask for word
        print_mask( mask );                // show mask
```

```
      do                    // do for each word to be guessed
      {
         letter = get_letter( );
         if (letter_in_word( word, letter ))
               update_mask( word, mask, letter );
         else {
               ++count;
               print_hangman( count );
         }
         print_mask( mask );

      } while (( !hangman_complete( count )) &&
                       ( !letters_all_found( mask )));
      if (hangman_complete( count ))
            cout << "\n\nI won - you lost!";
      else cout << "\n\nWell done! You found the word!";
      cout << "\n\nPlay? Answer yes/no: ";
      reply = get_letter( );
   } while ( ( reply == 'y' ) || ( reply == 'Y' ) );
}                       // end of main function definition

// other function definitions

// function that returns a character input from keyboard
char get_letter( )
{
   char ch;
   cout << "\nLetter please: ";
   cin >> ch;
   cin.ignore( LINE_LENGTH, '\n' );
   return ch;
}

/* function that constructs a mask s2 for a constant
                word s1, arguments are word and mask */
void initial_mask( const char* s1, char* s2 )
{
   const char* p = s1;
   char* q = s2;

   for ( ; *p != EOS ; p++, q++ )
      *q = '-';

   *q = EOS;
}

/* function that writes current state of mask,
                                    argument is mask */
void print_mask( const char* s2 )
{
   cout << "\nMask is \t\t\t\t" << s2 << endl;
}
```

```
/* function that returns TRUE if letter is in word else
   returns FALSE, arguments are word s1 and letter ch */

int letter_in_word( const char* s1, char ch )
{
   const char* p = s1;
   for ( ;  *p != EOS ; p++ )
     if ( ch == *p )  return TRUE;
          // end if and when letter first occurs in word
   return FALSE;      // end when no occurrence of letter
}


/* function that places correctly guessed letter ch
   of word s1 into corresponding positions in mask s2,
                  arguments are word, mask, and letter */

void update_mask( const char* s1, char* s2, char ch )
{
   const char* p = s1;
   char* q = s2;
   for ( ;  *p != EOS ; p++, q++ )
     if ( ch == *p )  *q = ch;
   cout << "Good";
}

// function that writes count letters of HANGMAN

void print_hangman( int count )
{
   char hangman[ ] = "HANGMAN";
   cout << "\nYou are hanging the man . . . ";
   for ( int i = 0; i < count; i++)
     cout.put( hangman[i] );
}

/* returns TRUE if all the letters in mask s2 are
        guessed else returns FALSE, argument is mask */

int letters_all_found( const char* s2 )
{
   const char* q = s2;
   for ( ;  *q != EOS ; q++ )
     if ( *q == '-' ) return FALSE;
                // end if and when an unguessed letter
   return TRUE;        // end if no hyphens found in mask
}
```

The next chapter will improve the playing of the game! We will alter the obvious deficiency that the player inputs the word that she/he guesses, and also extend the game to guess phrases rather than single words.

5.6.6 *The output and input of single characters*

The program shows several new ways of handling input and output with **cin** and **cout**. It introduces the concept that the standard output stream **cout** is an instance (object) of **ostream**, the class of output streams and that the standard input stream **cin** is an instance of **istream**, the class of input streams. Because of this, we can select *member functions* of these classes to handle these instances.

The *print_hangman( )* function outputs a specified count of single letters of the string literal "HANGMAN". We can use the *member function* **put( )** of the **ostream** class to output a single letter. The prototype of **put( )** is:

        ostream& put (char ch) ;

This function inserts a character **ch** into an output stream. The return_type **ostream&** means that an **ostream** reference is returned by the function.

A member function of a class can be selected in the same way as a member of a struct (see 4.7). An instance (object) of that class is used with the direct selection (dot) operator to access a class member. So, in *print_hangman( )*, the **ostream** instance **cout** is used with the **ostream** member function **put( )** in the statement

        cout.put (hangman[i]) ;

to insert the ith char of "HANGMAN" into the standard output buffer.

The function *get_letter( )* shows how one char can be extracted from possibly several chars in a line. *get_letter( )* uses **cin** to read in a char from the keyboard using the statement

        cin >> ch; .

We need to make the read ignore any more characters put in the buffer until the newline character is met, and also ignore the newline character itself. We select the *member function* **ignore( )** of **istream**. The declaration of **ignore( )** is

        istream& ignore (int len, int delim) ;

This function extracts and discards chars until it encounters the delimiter, *delim*, which is also extracted and discarded; *len* is the maximum number of characters that will be ignored. So in *get_letter( )* the two statements

        cin >> ch;
        cin.ignore (LINE_LENGTH, '\n') ;

will read in a single character and discard any other characters typed in on that line, including newline.

An alternative method of extracting a single character is to use the **istream** member function **get( )**. The prototype of **get( )** is

        istream& get (char& ch) ;

This extracts a single character **ch** from the input stream. So in *get_letter( )* we could have used the statements

        cin.get (ch) ;
        cin.ignore (LINE_LENGTH, '\n') ;

to read in a single character and discard any other characters typed in on that line, including the newline character.

5.7 The scope, visibility, and duration of an identifier

The *scope* of an identifier is that part of a program in which the identifier can be used to access its associated object. There are five categories of scope in C++: *block* (or *local*), *function*, *function prototype*, *file*, and *class*.

The *visibility* of an identifier is that part of a program from which legal access can be made to the identifier's associated object.

The *duration* of an identifier defines the period during which an identifier has an associated data object which is actually allocated storage in memory. There are three kinds of duration: *static, local,* and *dynamic*.

The scope, visibility, and duration of an object usually coincide, although there are circumstances in which they differ.

5.7.1 Scope

The scope of an identifier depends on how and where the identifier is defined.

Block or *local* scope is the scope of an identifier defined in a declaration statement within a block: an *enclosing* block. The scope of the identifier *starts at the declaration* and *extends to the end of the block*; for example, consider the identifier **count** defined in the block of the outer **do** statement in the **main** function of the hangman program
```
{ . . .    int count = 0;   . . . }
```
The scope of **count** begins with the declaration statement and extends to the closing brace. It is redeclared and initialised every time the **do** statement is re-entered (for every new word to be guessed).

Block or *local* scope also enables the same identifier to refer to different data objects in different blocks. For example, in the program **p** is defined within *initial_mask( )* and within *update_mask( )*: the two definitions of **p** cause the identifier to refer to two unrelated objects. These objects are separate copies of the **word** that 'exist' at different times. The two definitions do not conflict and statements in *update_mask( )* do not refer to the identifier **p** declared in *initial_mask( )*, and vice versa.

The only identifiers having *function scope* are *statement labels*. Label names can be used with **goto** statements anywhere in the function in which the label is declared. Label names are declared by *label_name: statement*. You are not encouraged to use this!

The formal argument *type* identifiers declared within an argument list in a function definition (and a function prototype) have *function prototype* scope. The scope of the type identifiers extends through the body of that function definition. The **char** type identifier declared in the argument lists of *letter_in_word( )* and *update_mask()* has this form of scope, for example.

Identifiers with *file* scope are defined outside of all blocks and classes; their scope is from the declaration statement, in which they are defined, to the end of the file. For example, in the previous program, the enumeration constant identifiers TRUE and FALSE have file scope and are used to access the constants of 1 and 0 throughout the *game1* program.

Class scope is considered further in Chapter 7.

5.7.2 Visibility cannot exceed scope, but scope can exceed visibility

Blocks can be nested, and a declaration in an inner block can hide a declaration of the same identifier in an enclosing block. For example, consider

```
{     . . .
   int count = 1;
   {
      . . .  int count = 0;   . . .
   }
}
```

Here, each declaration of **count** is associated with a different data object; the declaration in the inner block hides the object declared in the outer block. Anywhere in the scope for the inner declaration, **count** refers to the integer object with an initial value of 0, the other integer object still exists but is 'invisible'. The identifier cannot be used to access the integer object with an initial value of 1 until the scope of the duplicate identifier is ended.

5.7.3 Duration

The duration of an object is the time during which it has storage allocated in memory. The duration of an object is also known as its *extent*.

Objects with *static* duration are allocated memory as soon as execution of a program module is underway. Objects with file scope have static duration. Static duration objects are initialised to zero (or null) in the absence of any explicit initialiser and are given storage in fixed data areas (or data segments).

Local duration objects, also known as *automatic* objects, have a more precarious existence. They are given storage on the *stack* (or in a *register*) when the enclosing block or function is entered. Storage is deallocated when the program exits that block or function. Local duration objects must be explicitly initialised, otherwise their contents are unpredictable. Local duration objects always have local scope. All of our objects in the example hangman program were of local duration, except for the constants declared before the main function. For example, the declaration of **count** within the **while** statement means that it has a separate existence for each of the times the game is played.

Dynamic duration objects are created and destroyed by specific function calls or operators during program execution. They are allocated storage from a special memory area, the *free store* or *heap*. Objects with dynamic duration are discussed further in Chapter 9.

5.8 The conditional operator ?:

A conditional operator, using the two symbols **?** and **:**, is used in a conditional expression of the form:
```
     expression-c ? expression-t : expression-f
```
which is similar in effect to the statement
```
     if (expression-c) expression-t else expression-f
```
If the condition in *expression-c* is true, *expression-t* is evaluated, if it is false then *expression-f* is evaluated and returned as the value of the expression.

For example, if **i**, **j**, and **k** have all been declared then the expression
```
     ( i > j ) ? k = 4 : k = 5
```
evaluates the assignment expression **k = 4** if **i** is greater than **j**, otherwise it evaluates the expression **k = 5**.

5.9 Program arguments

We can pass arguments to a C++ program at run-time, when it is to be executed. Environments provide different ways for doing this (see Appendix 1).

When arguments are passed to a program the **main( )** function itself needs to be defined with formal arguments. It takes two formal arguments, as shown in:
```
     void main( int argc, char* argv[ ] )
```
where **argc** is the number of arguments including the program identifier, and **argv** is a pointer to an array of strings each of which is an argument.

The first string in the array argv[ ] is the program identifier, and all of the strings are normally separated by white space.

5.9.1 An example program which echoes all of its arguments except the first

This example program behaves like a simple form of the Unix and DOS *echo* commands:

```
// file echo echoes command line arguments
#include <iostream.h>

void main( int argc, char* argv[ ] )
{
   for ( int i = 1; i < argc; i++ )
     cout << argv[i] << ((i < (argc - 1 )) ? ' ' : '\n');
}
```

Suppose the command line to execute this program is
```
echo hello world
```
Each word on the line is an argument and the program identifier is **echo**. The output is
```
hello world
```

For this command line, **argc** is 3 since there are three command line arguments, and the string components of **argv** are assigned as:

```
argv[ 0 ] =  "echo"
argv[ 1 ] =  "hello"
argv[ 2 ] =  "world"
```

The **for** statement will use the values for **i** of 1 and 2, writing out the second and third argument strings. On the first repetition of the statement, after **hello** is inserted into the output stream, the conditional expression

```
(( i < ( argc - 1 )) ? ' ' : '\n' )
```

evaluates to the space character ' ' which is then inserted into the output stream. On the second repetition of the **for** statement, after **world** is inserted, the conditional expression evaluates to the newline character which completes the output.

Notice also in this example program that the count for the argument strings subscript **i** is declared when it is needed - in the initialisation expression of the **for** statement.

Exercises for Chapter 5

1. Use the technique of functional decomposition to develop a program which simulates the throws of two dice. Each dice has six faces and each face shows one of the values from 1 to 6. Assume the dice are not loaded so that, at each throw, a random number between 1 and 6 is obtained. For each throw, the total of the two uppermost faces is found, giving a total in the range from 2 to 12.

The program should input the number of throws to be simulated, and output the numbers of all the totals obtained. (For large numbers of throws, the numbers of the totals should show a normal distribution.)

2. Write a program that will accept run-time arguments and uses functions from the **string** library, where appropriate, to:

write out the number of run-time arguments,

echo any run-time arguments that include the *q* character,

echo any run-time arguments that start with the letters *test*,

echo any run-time arguments that end with *.doc*.

3. A bookshop manager keeps details of the Author, Title, Publisher, and Price for each of the books in stock in a shop. Write a program for the bookshop manager that gives the manager a menu so that:

the details of up to ten books can be entered,

all the details recorded can be written out,

if a title is given, the other details of a book are written out,

if an author is given, the details of all the author's books in stock are written,

if a publisher is given, the details of all the publishers books in stock are written,

the current total value of all the books is written out.

6 Data files and library files

We have entered our programs, using a keyboard and an editor, as *text files*: as streams of (ASCII) bytes. Any text entered using editors or word-processors will be stored as text files. We can use an editor to create text *data files*. We first consider, in this chapter, *extracting* (and *inserting*) data objects from (and to) data file streams.

This chapter also shows how we can create our own libraries. To execute our program files we have *compiled* and then *linked* them before running them. When a program file in C++ is compiled, all the **include**d library *header* files are inserted (pasted) into the file and compiled with the rest of the text.

Each *header* file has an associated *implementation* file. This library implementation file must be also compiled. A program file and a library implementation file are separate *compilation units*.

When a compiled program file is linked, it is linked to all the compiled implementation files that contain the definitions needed to implement the included header files.

6.1 Handling data file streams

In our programs so far we have used the standard input stream, from the keyboard, **cin**, and the standard output stream, to the screen, **cout**. These are both objects of the **iostream** classes, and use the operators >> and << (respectively) and the member functions (such as **ignore( )**, **get( )**, and **put( )**) defined by those classes (see 5.6.6).

For accessing data files we use the classes of **fstream** *which inherit operators and member functions from* **iostream**. So we can use the operators and member functions that we have already encountered, but we must usually **include iostream.h** whenever we **include fstream.h**.

The virtual base class of **iostream** is **ios**, from which we use some constants. (Chapter 11 discusses virtual base classes, and Appendix 5 shows the **ios** family inheritance diagram.)

6.1.1 Declaring a stream, and opening a file

We declare a file stream object either for input, or for output, or for both, using:
```
ifstream fidentifier;
```
when *fidentifier* is to be an input stream,
```
ofstream fidentifier;
```
when *fidentifier* is to be an output stream, and
```
fstream fidentifier;
```
when *fidentifier* is to be used as either an input or an output stream.

fidentifier is the name by which the file will be known by *our program*.

When we open a file, and attach it to a stream, we give the *filename* and specify the mode in which the file is to be opened. The *filename* is a string and is the name by which the file is known to the *operating system*.

A file mode is represented by one or more **ios** constants, of which the following are the most widely used:

ios :: in   which allows data to be read from a file,

ios :: out   which allows data to be written to a file, from the beginning, overwriting any data in the file, and

ios :: app   which allows data to be written to a file, appending it to the end of the existing data.

For both of the output modes, the named file will be created, if it does not yet exist. A file can then be opened using the **fstream** member function **open( )** in a statement of the form:

```
fidentifier . open( filename, ios :: mode );
```

Example statements showing how an input file can be declared and initialised

```
ifstream inFile;
                // declaring an ifstream object inFile
inFile.open( "data.txt", ios :: in );
                // opening the file as an input stream
```

The declaration of an **fstream** object, and opening a named file as that object (initialisation) can also be done in a single statement; the two statements above could be rewritten as:

```
ifstream inFile( "data.txt", ios :: in );
```

6.1.2 Closing a file stream

When a data file is no longer needed during program execution, it should be closed using the **fstream** member function **close( )**. For example, the statement:

```
inFile.close( );
```

will close the file *data.txt* opened by the statements given above.

6.1.3 Reading from and writing to data files

To read from or write to data files we can use the operators and member functions that we use with the **iostream** objects **cin** and **cout**. We replace these objects with *fidentifier*, the identifier of the **fstream** object that has been declared. For example, in the example program *game2*, shown in 6.2, a word for the player to guess is read in from a line in a data file using the statements:

```
inFile >> word;
inFile.ignore( LINE_LENGTH, '\n' );
```

The member functions **get( )** and **getline( )** can also be used to read from **inFile**.

Data objects can be inserted into an output file stream in a similar way. The *fidentifier* of the output file is used instead of **cout**, where required.

6.1.4 iostream condition state member functions

For each **iostream** (and therefore **fstream**) class object a set of condition flags
is maintained, through which the ongoing state of the stream can be monitored.
The four member functions returning the state of the flags are given in
Appendix 5. The program examples in this book only use the function **eof( )**
which returns *true* if the stream has reached *end_of_file*.

Example statement using eof( ) in the example program game2
```
    if (  inFile.eof( )  )                  // if end_of_file
       {
            cout << "Sorry, no more words in file";
            break;   // go to end of enclosing block
       }
```

6.1.5 Using a data file as a program argument

It is frequently useful to give the data file to be used as a run-time argument
(see 5.8) so that different data files can be used as required. For example, in
game2, the hangman game becomes a real one if the player can be provided with
a choice of words from different files, such as *animals.txt* or *towns.txt*, when the
player runs the game. So in *game2* the words come from a file given as the
second run-time argument with the following statements:
```
    ifstream inFile;
    inFile.open( argv[1], ios :: in );
```

6.2 The second version of the hangman game using a data file

The following version is a great improvement on the previous version, from the
point of view of the player. The words are now input from a data file, so it
becomes a true guessing game. A player can be given a choice of word lists by
using a different data file as a program argument each time the program is run.

The program is very similar to the first version, shown in full in 5.6.5.
The difference between the first and second version is only in how the words to
be guessed are obtained from a data file given as a program argument.

Only the revised **main( )** function definition of *game2* is given here; the
directives and declarations at the head of the program are the same as those in
game1 in 5.6.5, as are the other functions definitions.

```
void main(int argc, char* argv[ ] )
{
   char word[ MAX_WORD + 1 ], mask[ MAX_WORD + 1 ];
   char letter, reply;
   ifstream inFile;                // infile is fidentifier
   inFile.open( argv[1], ios::in );    // open data file
```

```
do                         // for each play of the game
  {
    inFile >> word;              // read a word from file
    inFile.ignore( LINE_LENGTH, '\n');
    if ( inFile.eof( ) )             // if end of file
      {
        cout << "Sorry, no more words in file";
        break;
      }
    int count = 0;
    initial_mask( word, mask );
    print_mask( mask );
    do
      {
        letter = get_letter( );
        if (letter_in_word( word, letter ))
            update_mask( word, mask, letter );
        else     {
                   ++count;
                   print_hangman( count );
                 }
        print_mask( mask );
      } while (( !hangman_complete( count ))
                    && ( !letters_all_found( mask ) ));
    if ( hangman_complete( count ) )
        cout << "\n\nI won - you lost!";
    else cout << "\n\nWell done! You found the word!";
    cout << "\n\nPlay again? Answer yes/no: ";
    reply = get_letter( );
  } while ( ( reply =='y' ) || ( reply == 'Y' ) );
  inFile.close();                    // close data file
}
```
// the following function definitions are the same as in *game1* in 5.6.5

6.3 Creating user-defined libraries

Each library consists of two files: a *header file*, and an *implementation file*.
In C++, when a library is to be used, the *library header file* is **included** at the
beginning of a program file ('pasted' in by the preprocessor). This means that *the
header file is compiled as part of the program file.*

The C++ compiler distinguishes between system-provided libraries and user-
defined libraries since system-provided libraries are stored in a directory known
to the compiler when the system is set up. A system-provided library header file
is enclosed between angular brackets when using the **#include** directive, for
example **#include <iostream.h>**, which we have used in every program.

The files of a user library can be stored in whichever directory the user
chooses, but the header pathname may have to be given to the compiler in the
#include directive.

The compiler needs to be aware that a user-defined library will not be stored with the system-provided libraries, so a user library header file name is enclosed between double quotes in an **#include** directive, for example:

```
#include "mylib.h"
```

This ensures that the preprocessor of the compiler goes to the correct directory to find a header file. (Much of the time occupied in compiling a module is taken up by the compilation of the header files included within them!)

A *library implementation file* is separately compiled. Its filename has the same extension as a program file, and the compiler will translate it into an object file in the same way as it translates an ordinary program file into an object file.

When a program object file is *linked* (before the program is run), it is linked to the implementation object files corresponding to the header files that have been included in the program.

Many C++ language environments, such as Unix, or Turbo C++, provide a *make* programming tool that will compile a program file and all the associated implementation files, and then link all the object files together ready for execution (ready to be run) if no syntax errors have been found. These tools should be explored with the next example program and its user-defined library - they make compilation much simpler! (See Appendix 1.)

6.3.1 Libraries

Each library should contain related definitions of functions and types (and classes) that form a logically homogeneous group. Each library should be as concise as possible.

The header file of a library provides the *interface* of the library, and gives the function declarations (function prototypes) and other definitions that may be used by programs. For example, by including the header file of **stdlib** in the example program shown in 2.11.1, we ensured that the functions **srand( )** and **rand( )** were declared before use in the main function of that program.

The header file is often used as a 'mini user guide': the purpose of each function can be explained in comments, and typical usage can be illustrated. Since a header file is often all that is available to a programmer (the source code for the implementation file may not be supplied), it is a natural place for the user to seek help in understanding how to use the functions.

The implementation file of a library is hidden from a program: a program has no knowledge of how a function is defined, and has no knowledge, either, of any data objects that are declared only within an implementation file.

6.4 The third version of the hangman game with a user library

This version illustrates how a *user-defined library* can be written. The game itself is unchanged for the player from the second version.

In this third version, a library, **mymask,** is used to hold the definitions and declarations for the data object **mask** and all the functions which handle it.

The header file of the library, **mymask.h,** holds the declarations of the functions which a program can use to handle a **mask.** These are *initial_mask( )*, *print_mask( )*, *update_mask( )*, and *letters_all_found( )*. These functions have been slightly rewritten so that **mask** is no longer an argument.

All the information about **mask** itself is hidden in the implementation file of the library. A program has no knowledge of it. **mask** is defined again as an array of chars and is declared as an object with file scope in the implementation file before any function definitions, so that all the functions defined in that file may access it.

The implementation file holds the definitions of all the functions whose function prototypes appear in the header file of the library.

6.4.1 The library header file

This contains the definitions, declarations, and function prototypes (function declarations) of functions that may be used by a program:

```
// file mymask.h, the library header file

const MAX_WORD = 20;
    // max. length of word for which a mask can be made
void initial_mask( const char* );
                        // forms a mask for a word
void print_mask( );         // writes the current mask
void update_mask( const char*, char );
        // uses word to insert a letter into a mask
int letters_all_found( );
            /* returns TRUE if letters all found in mask
                            else returns FALSE */
```

6.4.2 The library implementation file

This contains the definition and declaration of **mask** and definitions of functions whose prototypes are given in the header file. It is compiled before being linked to the program module. Its name has the same extension as that of a program file.

```
/* file mymask, the corresponding library implementation
                            file */
#include <iostream.h>

const EOS = '\0';
const MAX_WORD = 20;
enum boolean { FALSE, TRUE };

char mask[ MAX_WORD + 1 ];
```

```
void initial_mask( const char* s1 )
{
   const char* p = s1;
   char* q = mask;
   for ( ; *p != EOS ; p++, q++ )
      *q = '-';
   *q = EOS;
}

void print_mask( )
{ cout << "\nMask is \t\t\t\t" << mask << endl;    }

void update_mask( const char* s1, char ch )
{
   const char* p = s1;
   char* q = mask;
   for ( ; *p != EOS ; p++, q++ )
      if ( ch == *p )  *q = ch;
   cout << "Good";
}

int letters_all_found( )
{ const char* q = mask;
   for ( ; *q != EOS ; q++ )
      if ( *q == '-' ) return FALSE;
   return TRUE;
}
```

6.4.3 The program that plays the hangman game

This version of the program accesses the user library functions. The other functions are unchanged and are defined after the **main( )** function as before. This program does not use a **mask** object directly, but only through the functions provided by the **mymask** library.

```
// file game3 with a user-defined library
#include <iostream.h>
#include <fstream.h>
#include "mymask.h"

const EOS = '\0';
const LINE_LENGTH = 80;
enum boolean { FALSE, TRUE };

// declarations of functions defined in this file
char get_letter( );
int letter_in_word( const char*, char );
void print_hangman( int );
inline int hangman_complete( int count )
{ return ( count == 7 )    }
```

```
void main(int argc, char* argv[ ] )
{
   char word[ MAX_WORD + 1 ];
   char letter, reply;
   ifstream inFile;
   inFile.open( argv[1], ios::in );
   do
     {
       inFile >> word;
       inFile.ignore( LINE_LENGTH, '\n');
       if ( inFile.eof( ) )
          {
             cout << "Sorry, no more words in file";
             break;
          }
       int count = 0;
       initial_mask( word );
       print_mask( );
       do
         {
             letter = get_letter( );
             if (letter_in_word( word, letter ))
               update_mask( word, letter );
             else    {
                     ++count;
                     print_hangman( count );
                  }
             print_mask( );
       } while (( !hangman_complete( count ))
                           && ( !letters_all_found( )));
       if (hangman_complete( count ))
           cout << "\n\nI won - you lost!";
       else cout << "\n\nWell done! You found the word!";
       cout << "\n\nPlay again? Answer yes/no: ";
       reply = get_letter( );
     } while ( ( reply =='y' ) || ( reply == 'Y' ) );
   inFile.close();
}
```
// the function definitions for those functions defined in this file are the same as
shown in *game1* in 5.6.5

6.5 Encapsulation and implementation hiding

In the preceding example, the library **mymask** is a *data capsule*. A *data capsule*
is a library which consists of the definition and declaration of data objects and a
collection of functions which manage these data objects. Some of these functions
are available for use by programs and other libraries, these are *access functions*.
The data itself, and all functions which are not access functions, are not
accessible from outside the capsule.

The binding of a data object (here **mask**) with an associated set of functions that can be used to manipulate this data object is called *encapsulation*; the inaccessibility of knowledge of the structure of the data object and the definitions of the functions is called *implementation hiding*.

mask, itself, is *an abstract data structure*. Such a structure can be defined as a set of data components and a set of functions (operations) which can be applied to the components or to the data structure as a whole for which the implementation details are hidden.

In many of the earlier programming languages there was relatively little check on the scope and visibility of data objects: a program consisted of one file, and a data object could be passed as an argument to any function. If changes were made to the structure of a data object there was no easy way of ensuring that all the functions that might be affected were found and altered accordingly. There were no compilation checks to enforce any necessary changes in function definitions that might handle the data object.

Also, when large programs were developed in such languages by software teams, each group of a team could not have a clear view of the interface of their section of code with that of others. A single program file is not easy to break down into discrete sections.

Moreover, a section of program code already developed, that is known to perform a subtask correctly, should be used when that subtask is encountered again. But, in these earlier languages, such a section must be rewritten into the file, and there is no mechanism to stop changes corrupting that rewritten section.

With encapsulation, using user-defined libraries, these problems can be overcome. The capsule that defines a data object also defines the functions that provide access to it. No other functions, outside the capsule, may handle it. This limits the sources of error arising from the way it is handled, and facilitates testing of alterations in the structure of the data object.

The interface of a capsule is given in the header file: only the definitions, data objects, and functions that are specifically declared in the header file, can be used by programs. This facilitates team development since each group can develop a separate capsule and all the other groups in the team know what is available for use in the capsule from its header file. The implementation of the capsule is hidden from the rest of the team, who cannot alter that implementation.

Finally, a capsule, as a library, may be reused at any time, its interface is known, and its implementation cannot be altered by the using program.

Exercises for Chapter 6

1. Amend the program produced for the bookshop manager (Exercises for Chapter 5, Exercise 3) so that all the details for the books held in stock may be held in a data file. The menu should also then provide the bookshop manager with the choices of writing all the details into the data file and of reading all the details from the data file.

2. Create a library that defines and declares a single struct *tel_record* whose data members are *name* and an unsigned integer *telephone_number*. Provide access functions to enable values for both the data members to be read into the *tel_record*, to write out the the the *tel_record*, to change just the value in the *name*, and to change just the value in *telephone_number*.

Write a program with a menu of choices to use each of the access functions. Use a *make* command to compile and then link the program and library implementation files (Appendix 1 gives details of how this is done with Unix and with Borland's Turbo C++).

7 Classes and derived classes

We have seen how to define and declare one data object as an abstract data structure. It would be more interesting to be able to define an abstract data structure so that any number of objects could be declared with this structure.

Such is *an abstract data type*, which defines the data structure of a set of data objects and the functions and operators applicable to them. In C++ an abstract data type is provided by a *class* whose implemetation details are usually hidden in a library.

In C++, users can define their own data type with a *class definition*. We can declare *(construct)* an actual *class object*. A class object is often called an *instance* of that class. A class object may have certain operations applied to it: the operations are given as *member functions* within the definition. A class object is handled using its associated member functions. One of the member functions is a *constructor function* that declares and can initialise a class object.

The type of a class object is given by the *class identifier* in the class definition. The components (structure) of a class object are given by the *data members* within the definition.

Both member functions and the data members of a class may be specified as **private, protected,** or **public**. These protection specifiers control the access to these members. Typically, the data members of a class are **private** while the member functions are **public**.

A member function has full access to both the public and private members of the class in which it is defined, while ordinary functions only have access to the public members of the class. The public members of the class are the *public interface* of the class.

This chapter also shows how we can define a new class by extending or modifying one or more existing classes. This is known as *inheritance*, because the new class inherits many of its members from the existing class or classes. Inheritance makes it easy to customise a class for a particular purpose.

7.1 Defining a class

A class definition is often held in a header file so that the definition is available for any program file that may wish to declare objects of that class.

The form of a class definition is:

```
class class_identifier
{
    data members ;
    member functions ;
} ;                          // note the concluding semi-colon after the curly brace
```

where members can be given **private, protected** or **public** levels of protection.

7.1.1 Data members

The data members give the structure of the data objects of a class. Indeed, the data members are similar to the data members of a **struct** and are accessed with the same selection operators.

However, a class can have far more features than a struct. We start by considering the *member functions* of a class. These members can also be accessed with the selection operators.

7.1.2 Defining member functions

The class definition usually holds the function prototypes of its member functions. The full definitions of the member functions are usually given in the corresponding implementation file to a library header file containing the class definition.

Inline member function definitions may be given fully in the class definition but, in this case, the keyword **inline** does not have to precede an inline definition.

The full definition of a member function is modified in the first line using the *scope resolution operator,* ::, as in:

```
return_type class_identifier :: fn_identifier(arguments)
```

The operator's left operand is a *class_identifier* and its right operand is a *function_identifier*. The scope resolution operator has a higher precedence than that of any other operator. It enables the same *function_identifier* to be used by different classes, or with no class association.

The definition of *function_identifier* which is tied to the scope of *class_identifier* enables this definition to be used with the same scope as a *class_identifier* object, and to have special privileges and access to the members of *class_identifier*.

An example of a member function definition from the **maskclass** library given in 7.3.1 is:

```
void mask :: print_mask( )
{
    cout << "\nMask is\t\t\t\t" << maskdata << endl;
}
```

The use of the scope operator makes this definition the one that is bound to objects of class **mask** - this definition has the same *scope* as objects of the class. A member function has *class scope*.

This function has the privilege of being able to access directly the other members of the class. So the data member, the **maskdata** string, of the mask class can be accessed using its identifier when required within the function definition.

7.1.3 Defining constructor member functions

Classes usually have at least one *constructor* member function which can be used
to *declare* (create) and possibly *initialise* an object of that class. The definition of
a constructor member function is similar to that of a general member function
except that a *constructor function_identifer* is a *class_identifier*, and a *constructor
function does not have a return_type.*

An example of the definition of a constructor which can be used to declare
and initialise a **mask** is shown in the **maskclass** library given in 7.3.2. Except for
the header line of the definition, it is the same as the *initial_mask( )* definition
given in the **mask** library of the third version of the game shown in 6.4.2.
The constructor uses its argument *word*, s1, to initialise a new **mask** object.

```
mask :: mask( const char* s1 )
{
   const char* p = s1;
   char* q = maskdata;
   for ( ; *p != EOS; p++, q++ )
      *q = '-';
   *q = EOS;
}
```

An object created using a class constructor is often referred to as an *instance*
of a class. Each instance created with the constructor shown here is the mask for
the word passed as an argument to the constructor.

7.1.4 Defining destructor member functions

A class object can be *destructed* using a member function called a *destructor*.
Since class objects with local scope are destructed at the end of the block in
which they are declared, it is not often essential to define a destructor function.
But if one is needed, its definition is similar to that of a constructor function
except that *a destructor function_identifer* is *class_identifier* preceded by a
tilde, ~, (~*class_identifier*). A destructor function also does not have a
return_type.

7.2 Handling class objects

Programs and other functions may declare class objects in the same way that we
have already declared objects of the predefined and derived types. The
class_identifier can be used where we have previously used *type* in a declaration.

Access to **public** members, by a program, is made by using the selection
operators.

7.2.1 Declarations and the scope of class objects

Consider the two declarations made in the middle of the **do** block in the *game4* program file shown in 7.3.3:

```
int count = 0;
mask m = word;
```

The first declaration creates and initialises the integer object **count**, we have seen this many times already and know that this object is destructed at the end of the **do** block since it has *block scope*. The second declaration creates and initialises the mask object (instance) with the identifier of **m**, using the constructor function of the class **mask**. This object is also destructed at the end of the block. When the **do** block is re-entered, two new objects are created when the declarations are met again.

The scope, visibility, and duration of class object identifiers obey the same rules as those for the identifiers of objects of the predefined and derived types.

7.2.2 Accessing public members

Programs and functions may access **public** members of a class using the direct and indirect selection operators, except when accessing a constructor or a destructor. The *game4* program uses the direct selection (dot) operator to access the public functions of the mask class several times. Consider the statements:

```
m.update_mask( word, letter );
m.print_mask( );
m.letters_all_found( );
```

In each case, the direct selection operator has a left operator of *class_object_identifier*, and a right operand of *class_member_function_identifier*. This is exactly the same usage as that discussed in 6.1, say, where fstream class objects were handled with fstream member functions in statements such as:

```
inFile.ignore( LINE_LENGTH, '\0' );
```

The direct selection operator was introduced together with structs, which are classes with only public data members. So the usage here corresponds to the use of the operator shown in 4.7.1.

Instances of a class are handled only by member functions of that class or by overloaded operators defined within the class, or by friend functions. (Chapter 8 introduces overloading and friend functions.)

7.3 The fourth version of the hangman game showing the use of a class

This version has a user-defined library **maskclass** where class **mask** is defined. The program file *game4* uses the class to declare and handle masks.

Note that the string holding a mask, **maskdata**, is a **private** data member of a **mask** instance and is only accessible to **mask** member functions. It is completely inaccessible to any other function.

The program reads words from a data file as before, and the definitions of functions defined in the program file are unchanged from previous versions.

7.3.1 The header file containing the class definition

```
// file maskclass.h

const MAX_WORD = 20;  // longest acceptable word length

class mask
{
  private:
    char maskdata[ MAX_WORD + 1 ];          // data member
  public:
    mask( const char* );
                        // constructor of a mask for a word
    void print_mask( );              // writes current mask
    void update_mask( const char*, char );
                // uses word to insert letter into mask
    int letters_all_found( );
                /* returns TRUE if no more letters in mask
                            to guess, else returns FALSE */
};
```

7.3.2 The implementation file containing the class function definitions

```
// file maskclass
#include <iostream.h>
#include "maskclass.h"          // class definition needed

const EOS = '\0';
enum boolean { FALSE, TRUE };

// constructor member function definition
mask :: mask( const char* s1 )
{
  const char* p = s1;
  char* q = maskdata;

  for ( ; *p != EOS; p++, q++ )
    *q = '-';
  *q = EOS;
}

// other member function definitions
void mask :: print_mask( )
{
  cout << "\nMask is\t\t\t\t" << maskdata << endl;
}
```

```
void mask :: update_mask( const char* s1, char ch )
{
   const char* p = s1;
   char* q = maskdata;

   for ( ; *p != EOS; p++, q++ )
     if ( ch == *p ) *q = ch;
   cout << "Good";
}

int mask :: letters_all_found( )
{
   char* q = maskdata;

   for ( ; *q != EOS; q++ )
     if ( *q == '-' ) return FALSE;
   return TRUE;
}
```

7.3.3 The program file game4 using the class mask

```
// file game4 uses the mask class definition
#include <iostream.h>
#include <fstream.h>
#include "maskclass.h"
const EOS = '\0';
const LINE_LENGTH = 80;
enum boolean { FALSE, TRUE };

// function prototypes of functions defined in this file
char get_letter( );
int letter_in_word( const char*, char );
void print_hangman( int );
inline int hangman_complete( int count )
{  return ( count == 7 );  }

void main( int argc, char* argv[ ] )
{
   char word[ MAX_WORD + 1 ];
   char letter, reply;
   ifstream inFile;
   inFile.open( argv[ 1 ], ios::in );
   do
     {
       inFile >> word;
       inFile.ignore( LINE_LENGTH, '\n' );
       if ( inFile.eof( ) )
           {
              cout << "Sorry, no more words in file";
              break;
           }
```

```
        int count = 0;           // declaring an int object
        mask m = word;           // declaring a mask object
        m.print_mask( );   // using a class member function
        do
          {
            letter = get_letter( );
            if (letter_in_word( word, letter ))
                m.update_mask( word,letter );
            else
                {   ++count;
                  print_hangman( count );
                }
            m.print_mask( );
          }while ((!hangman_complete(count))
                          && (!m.letters_all_found( )));

        if (hangman_complete( count ))
          cout << "\n\nI won - you lost!";
        else cout << "\n\nWell done! You found the word!";

        cout << "\n\nPlay again? Answer yes/no: ";
        reply = get_letter( );
      } while ( ( reply == 'y' ) || ( reply == 'Y' ));
    inFile.close( );
}
```
// function definitions for functions defined in this file are as in *game1* in 5.6.5

7.4 Inheritance from a base class by a derived class

The class construct provides the logical unit of encapsulation in C++: each object of a class is constructed with its own set of data member values and can be manipulated using the public members given in the class definition.

The usefulness of such data encapsulation can be greatly enhanced if a class can be customised for another application by adding to, or changing members of that class. The feature of an *object-oriented language* that makes this possible is *inheritance*. Inheritance allows programmers to use an existing class in constructing a hierarchy of reusable software components.

The *derived class* construct in C++ is the basis for inheritance and provides the method for customising a base (parent) class. C++ allows a *derived* (child) *class to inherit or modify all the members of its base class* and, in addition, to provide itself *with new members* for the application in which it will be used.

A derived class cannot access the **private** members of its parent. It can access the **protected** and **public** members. All class members declared as **protected** are hidden in the same way as **private** members except with respect to derived classes. The protection modes for the members of classes are:

        private

when private members may only be accessed by other members of that class, and

```
        protected
```
when protected members may only be accessed by members of that class or a derived class, and
```
        public
```
when public members may be used by any function (the class *public interface*).

Diagrammatically, the relationship between a base (parent) class and a derived class is visualised as:

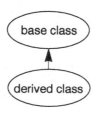

7.4.1 Defining a derived class using either a private or a public base class

Using differing protection modes for the base class gives differing protection to the **public** parts of that class. The *inheritance list* of a base class is given following a colon in the header line of the derived class definition.

When using a **private** base class the header line for the full definition of the derived class is:
```
class derived_class_identifier
                        : private base_class_identifier
```
The colon separating *base_class_identifier* from *derived_class_identifier* is used to establish the hierarchy between the subclass and its base classes. The inheritance list here contains one base class (*multiple inheritance* is discussed in Chapter 11).

With a **private** base class, *the protected and public members of the base class become private members of the derived class.* They can be accessed by member and friend functions of the derived class but *are not accessible to users of the derived class.*

We use a **private** base class if we need to provide a different set of members for users of the derived class and so want to block access to the members defined in the base class. By default, if no protection mode is specified for the base class, it is taken to be **private**.

The alternative form of the definition is one which allows objects of the derived class to use all of the members of the base class, unless these have been redefined in the derived class. The **public** members of the base class are also **public** members of the derived class. The header line for this form of the definition of the derived class is:
```
class derived_class_identifier
                        : public base_class_identifier
```

7.4.2 Constructors for derived classes

An object of a derived class is usually constructed from objects of the base classes. Because an object of a derived class may contain members from both the base classes and the derived class, constructors for both the base and the derived class must be used to initialise an object.

In the constructor for the derived class, the full function definition header line is followed by a colon and an *constructor initialisation list* that contains a call to a constructor for the base class. A constructor of the base class is given with an argument list that contains the identifiers of its formal arguments *without their types or classes*.

An example of a constructor for a derived class **maskphrase** is shown in the **phrase** library in 7.5.2. The constructor is derived from the **mask** constructor whose formal argument identifier is **s1**, so the initialisation list is **mask(s1)**. The constructor makes a mask for phrases (instead of just single words), and therefore puts spaces in the mask corresponding to spaces within the phrase:

```
maskphrase :: maskphrase( const char* s1 ) : mask( s1 )
{
    const char* p = s1;
    char* q = maskdata;              // maskdata is inherited

    for ( ; *p != EOS; p++, q++ )
       if ( *p == ' ' )
                *q = ' ';
        else    *q = '-';
    *q = EOS;
}
```

The creation of a base class object preceding that of the derived object can be seen quite clearly in this version of game if the function *print_mask( )* is inserted at the end of both the **mask** and the **maskphrase** constructor functions. For example, if the **phrase** is

        have a nice day
the statement in the program creating a **maskphrase** object:

        maskphrase m = phrase;
generates the output:

mask is   ---------------
mask is   ---- - ---- ---

The data member of the base class object here is a string of hyphens, the number of hyphens being the same as the number of characters in the input string *phrase*. The data member of the derived class object is then constructed and initialised as a string including space characters as well as hyphen characters.

7.4.3 Destructors for derived classes

Destructors are called in the reverse order to that of constructors: the destructor for a base class is called *after* the destructor of the derived class has been executed.

7.5 The fifth version of the hangman game showing class inheritance

Our versions of the game, so far, have not been able to cope with the input of more than one word or of the space character since the extraction operation stops at white space. An instance of the class **mask**, developed in the previous version in 7.3, is constructed with initial values of '−' (hyphens) in all the positions corresponding to the word string read in.

The fifth, and final, version of the game derives a class **maskphrase** from the class **mask**. The definition of class **mask** has been altered slightly: the data member **maskdata** is now **protected** (instead of **private**) so that it can be accessed by member functions of the derived class **maskphrase**.

The objects of **maskphase** inherit all of the members of **mask**. The member functions defined in **mask** can be used to handle **maskphrase** objects, so **mask** is made a **public** base class, and there is no need, in this case, for further member functions to be defined beyond a constructor function to create a **maskphrase**.

Phrases are read in from a data file using the **istream** member function **getline( )**, in the statement:

```
    inFile.getline( phrase, LINE_LENGTH, '\n' );
```

This reads a string of characters that may include spaces and tabs into *phrase* until either LINE_LENGTH is reached or the *newline* char is read.

7.5.1 The header file containing the base and derived class definitions

```
// file phrase.h

const MAX_WORD = 20;

class mask
{
   protected:        // derived class members have access
      char maskdata[ MAX_WORD + 1 ];
   public:                   // all functions may access
      mask( const char* );        // constructor function
      void print_mask( );
      void update_mask( const char*, char );
      int letters_all_found( );
};
```

```
class maskphrase : public mask
{
  public:                    // all functions may access
    maskphrase( const char* ); // constructor function
};
```

7.5.2 The implementation file containing the class member function definitions

```
// file phrase
#include <iostream.h>
#include "phrase.h"

const EOS = '\0';
enum boolean { FALSE, TRUE };

// class mask constructor function
mask :: mask( const char* s1 )
{
  const char* p = s1;
  char* q = maskdata;
  for ( ; *p != EOS; p++, q++)
    *q = '-';
  *q = EOS;
}

// other class mask member functions
void mask :: print_mask( )
{
  cout << "\nMask is\t\t\t\t" << maskdata << endl;
}

void mask :: update_mask( const char* s1, char ch )
{
  const char* p = s1;
  char* q = maskdata;
  for ( ; *p != EOS; p++, q++ )
    if ( ch == *p ) *q = ch;
  cout << "Good";
}

int mask :: letters_all_found( )
{
  char* q = maskdata;
  for ( ; *q != EOS; q++ )
    if ( *q == '-' ) return FALSE;
  return TRUE;
}
```

```
// class maskphrase constructor function
maskphrase :: maskphrase( const char* s1 ) : mask( s1 )
{
   const char* p = s1;
   char* q = maskdata;
   for ( ; *p != EOS; p++, q++ )
     if ( *p == ' ' ) *q = ' ';
     else    *q = '-';
   *q = EOS;
}
```

7.5.3 The program file using the derived class

```
// file game5 uses the maskphrase definition
#include <iostream.h>
#include <fstream.h>
#include "phrase.h"

const EOS = '\0';
const LINE_LENGTH = 80;
enum boolean { FALSE, TRUE };

// function prototypes of functions defined in this file
char get_letter( );
int letter_in_phrase( const char*, char );
void print_hangman( int );
inline int hangman_complete( int count )
{ return ( count == 7 );  }

void main( int argc, char* argv[ ] )
{
   char phrase[ MAX_WORD + 1 ];
   char letter, reply;
   ifstream inFile;
   inFile.open( argv[ 1 ], ios::in );
   do
     {
       inFile.getline( phrase, LINE_LENGTH, '\n' );
       if ( inFile.eof( ) )
           {
             cout << "Sorry, no more phrases in file";
             break;
           }

       int count = 0;
       maskphrase m = phrase;
          // declare and initialise derived class instance

       m.print_mask( );
```

```
   do
   {
      letter = get_letter( );
      if (letter_in_phrase( phrase, letter ))
           m.update_mask( phrase,letter );
      else    {
                    ++count;
                    print_hangman( count );
              }
      m.print_mask( );
   } while (( !hangman_complete( count))
                        && ( !m.letters_all_found( )));
   if (hangman_complete( count ))
      cout << "\n\nI won - you lost!";
   else cout << "\n\nWell done! You found the phrase!";
   cout << "\n\nPlay again? Answer yes/no: ";
   reply = get_letter( );
   } while ( ( reply == 'y' ) || ( reply == 'Y' ));
   inFile.close();
}
// function definitions as in previous version
```

Exercises for Chapter 7

1. Write the definition, in a header file, of a *tel_record* class whose data members are *name* (up to 30 characters), and an unsigned integer *telephone_number*, and whose member functions are *read( )* (reads a record details from data input from the keyboard), and *write( )* (writes out the details of an actual record to the screen). The constructor function will have an empty definition { }, since no initialisation will be performed when a record is declared.

   Write the corresponding implementation file which contains the full definitions of the member functions *read( )* and *write( )* of the *tel_record* class.

2. Write a program module which will read in up to ten different instances of class *tel_record*. Use an array of *tel_record*s. Finish by writing the records onto the screen in same order in which they were entered.

3. Derive, in a header file, a class *tel_directory* from the *tel_record* class so that the derived class objects have a further data member *address* (up to 70 characters). Write the corresponding implementation file that includes suitable new definitions for the member functions *read( )* and *write()*. When *tel_directory* objects are then used to select these member functions, the definitions of the functions associated with the *tel_directory* class are bound, by the compiler, to the program code.

   Write a program that gives a user a menu of actions giving a choice between entering up to a maximum of ten *tel_directory* entries, and writing the complete list of entries onto the screen.

8 Overloading and friends

Both functions and operators can be *overloaded* in C++. This means that several definitions can be associated with a function identifier or with most operator symbols.

For functions, this means that the same *function identifier* can be associated with several differing function definitions, all with the same scope. However, the *signature* (the types and number of arguments) of each of these definitions must be different. The compiler looks at the types and numbers of the actual arguments used in a call of such a function to determine which of the possible definitions associated with the function identifier should be bound to the code at the call.

Overloaded function definitions are not necessarily associated with classes.

Overloaded operator definitions are associated with classes. The operation associated with an operator symbol can be redefined for one or more operands that are class instances. An overloaded operator definition is given as a special form of a member or *friend* function of a class.

A *friend* has full access rights to the private and protected members of the class to which it is defined to be a friend. Friend functions are discussed in this chapter. In the next chapter, a friend class is used.

To illustrate overloading and friend functions, a **mystring** library is shown that defines a string in an alternative way to the standard **string** library. A new **mstring** class is provided that includes operators and functions to handle class objects. The program that uses this library is almost identical to the *playstr* program in 4.5.2. This new string class definition makes provision for an *exception* (a possible cause of a run-time error), and the program runs without the overwriting of strings problem that occurred with the earlier program.

8.1 Program example with overloading and friend functions

The **mystring** library defines new strings, **mstrings**, that are provided with extraction and insertion operator definitions so that they can be handled by iostream objects, and given two other operator definitions that enable similar facilities to **string** library functions. Some of these operators are provided as friend functions. There is also a simple friend function *length( )*.

These friend functions access **mstring** data members but do not alter any data member values. The concatenation operator symbol, + =, is given a new definition and is used to alter the data members of an **mstring**, this new definition is given as a full member function of the class.

Function overloading is used to provide three alternative **mstring** constructor functions. Each of these constructor function definitions have different argument types (or no arguments).

mstrings each have two data members; one is a char array (not necessarily terminated by the null character), and the other is an integer length. Both the constructor and the concatenation operator definitions ensure that no **mstring** exceeds the (fixed size) storage allocated to such a class object using the exception handling *error( )* function that is private to the class.

8.1.1 The header file mystring.h declaring the mstring class

```
// file mystring.h

const LEN_MAX = 79;      // maximum length of an mstring

class mstring
{
    private:   // an mstring object has two data members:
        int len;          // the count of chars in the array
        char p[ LEN_MAX ];                    // a char array
    public:                  // public member functions:
        mstring( ) {  len  =  0 ;   }
                    // a constructor of a null mstring
        mstring( const char* );
            // a constructor of an mstring from a string
        mstring( const mstring& );
        // a constructor of an mstring from another (copy)
        mstring& operator+= ( const mstring );
                    // appends one mstring to another
                                // friend functions:
    friend istream& operator>> ( istream&, mstring& );
            // extraction operator: extracts an mstring
    friend ostream& operator<<( ostream&, const mstring );
            // insertion operator: inserts an mstring
    friend int operator== ( const mstring, const mstring);
                // equality comparison operator
    friend int length( const mstring  s ){return  s.len;}
                // returns the length of an mstring
    private:                 // private member function:
        void error( );
        // prevents data member p from becoming too large
};
```

8.1.2 The corresponding implementation file for mstring.h

This holds the definitions of member and friend functions not defined inline.

```
// file mystring
#include <iostream.h>
#include <string.h>       // uses the strlen( ) function
#include <stdlib.h>        // uses the exit( ) function
#include "mystring.h"
```

```
// member function definitions
                // a constructor of an mstring from a string
mstring :: mstring( const char* str )
{
   if ( strlen( str ) > LEN_MAX )
      error( );                  // exit if storage exceeded
   len = strlen( str );   // else find length of mstring
   for ( int i = 0; i < len ; i++ )
      p[ i ] = str[ i ];
      // and put chars into array data member of mstring
}

   // a constructor of an mstring from another mstring s
mstring :: mstring( const mstring& s )
{
   len = s.len;
   for ( int i = 0; i < len ; i++ )
      p[ i ] = s.p[ i ];
}

                   // redefining the += operator symbol
mstring& mstring :: operator+= ( const mstring s )
{
   if (( len + s.len ) > LEN_MAX )
      error( );        // exit if storage would be exceeded
   for ( int i = 0; i < s.len ; i++ )
      p[ len + i ] = s.p[ i ];
   len += s.len;
   return *this;        // returns pointer to this mstring
}

/* exception handling: if necessary, causes orderly
                         termination of program */
void mstring :: error( )
{    cout << "\nString too large" << endl;  exit( 0 ); }

// friend function definitions
                // redefining the extraction operator
istream& operator>> ( istream& is, mstring& s )
{
   char buffer[ LEN_MAX ];
   is.getline( buffer, LEN_MAX, '\n' );
   s = mstring( buffer );
   return is;        // returns reference to input stream
}
                // redefining the insertion operator
ostream& operator<< ( ostream& os, const mstring s )
{
   for ( int i = 0; i < s.len ; i++ )
      os << s.p[i];
   return os;        // returns reference to output stream
}
```

```
                   // redefining the equality operator == symbol
int operator== ( const mstring s, const mstring t )
{
  if ( s.len != t.len )
    return 0;          // return FALSE if lengths differ
  for ( int i = 0; i < s.len ; i++ )
    if ( s.p[ i ] != t.p[ i ] )  return 0;
          // return FALSE if corresponding chars differ
  return 1;   // return TRUE if lengths and chars same
}
```

8.1.3 A program that uses the mystring library

This program is almost the same as the example program shown in 4.5.2 where concatenation of an input string **a** onto the string literal **reponse** overwrote another string literal at run-time. Here this problem is overcome using **mstrings** instead of strings since all the **mstring** objects have a fixed amount of storage allocated to them as each data member **p**, of an **mstring**, is allocated LEN_MAX **char** storage spaces when it is declared, even though only part of this storage space may be used. When two **mstrings** are concatenated (using the overloaded + = operator), the first action of the definition is to see whether their combined lengths exceeds the storage limit. If the combined lengths are too great then the *error( )* function will output a message and terminate program execution.

```
// file teststring
#include <iostream.h>
#include "mystring.h"

void main( )
{
  mstring message = "Enter a string: ";
  mstring response = "\nYour string is: ";
          // initialise mstrings from string literals
  mstring a, b;   // declaring two unitialised mstrings
  char ch;
  do
   {
     cout << message;
     cin >> a;                      // extracting an mstring
     response += a;      // using the redefined += symbol
     cout << response << endl;
          // inserting an mstring and a manipulator
     cout << "\nThe length of your string is: "
          << length( a );  // using a friend function
     cout << "\nInput a second string: ";
     cin >> b;
     mstring c = b;
          // declaring and initialising a new mstring
```

```
        if ( a == c )        // using the redefined == symbol
              cout << "\nBoth strings are the same";
        else    cout << "\nYour strings are different";
        cout << "\nPlay with strings? Answer yes or no: ";
        cin.get(ch); cin.ignore(80, '\n');
      } while ( ch == 'y' );
}
```

This time, each of the first strings entered, **a,** is appended in turn to the end of **response** until the storage is exceeded. The new definition of a string solves the concatenation problem by restricting the amount of storage allocated to one string. This storage is allocated by the compiler. If the exception handling function *error( )* is not provided, then the program will abnormally terminate at run-time if the amount of storage demanded for an object exceeds the amount allocated. The exception handling routine ensures that we obtain an abrupt, but normal, termination with a message indicating why that termination occurred.

The next chapter shows how storage can be allocated to objects at run-time.

8.2 Friends

Normally any function outside a class can only access the **public** members of a class instance. The construct of a **friend** allows this protection to be modified. One or more outside functions or an entire outside class can be declared to be a **friend** of a specific class. This declaration is made within that class definition. Such *a friend can then access the private and protected members of the class.*

8.2.1 Friend functions

Friend functions share most of the privileges of member functions but they are not as strongly committed to any one class: a function can be a friend of several classes, but it can be a member of at most one. (Just as a person can be a friend of many families, but a member of just one family.)

Constructors, destructors, and virtual functions (see Chapter 11) must be member functions. Apart from these, functions may be member functions or friend functions. However, there are conventions used by C++ programmers which give guidelines for making a decision on this. These conventions are discussed in 8.4 below.

A friend has access to the private and protected parts of all classes that have declared it as a friend. But it does not have the unqualified access given to member functions; to access a *class_member* its definition must specify the *class_object_identifier* as well, using a selection operator.

The friend function definitions given in the example library all use the direct selection (dot) operator to access members as in

   class_object_identifier . class_member.

Consider the simplest of the friend functions, defined inline:

```
friend int length( const mstring s ){ return s.len; }
```

This returns the length of the **mstring** object whose formal argument identifier is s, an argument passed by value. Since this function is a friend function, and not a member function, the definition selects the data member **len** of s using the object identifier and the direct selection operator.

8.3 Function overloading

C++ allows function identifiers, with the same scope, to be overloaded. This means that the same function identifier can be associated with several definitions. Each of these definitions must, however, have differing types of arguments, *a differing signature*.

The compiler, when translating, determines which function definition is to be used by the number and type of arguments that are used in the function call. The selected definition is bound to the code by the compiler. This is *early* (or *static*) *binding*.

8.3.1 Example of function overloading in the mstring class definition

Three constructor functions are defined within the class definition,

```
mstring( ) { len = 0 ; }
```

which is a constructor creating an empty *mstring*, and

```
mstring( const char* );
```

which is a constructor creating an *mstring* from a string, and

```
mstring( const mstring& );
```

which is a constructor forming and initialising a new *mstring* from an existing *mstring* (a copy constructor).

These three functions each have different argument lists but the same class scope and the same identifier **mstring**, so the function identifier is *overloaded*.

The first constructor function, **mstring( )**, has no arguments, and is defined inline. It is used in the program *teststring* in the declaration statement:

```
mstring a, b;
```

to create storage for two uninitialised class objects.

The second constructor function has one argument, a pointer with the char referenced type. It is used in the program in the declaration statements:

```
mstring message = "Enter a string: ";
mstring response = "\nYour string is: ";
```

These declarations construct instances (objects) of the **mstring** class from string literals, the string literals are used to initialise the instances.

This constructor is also used within the overloaded extraction operator definition in the **mystring** implementation file, in the statement:

```
s = mstring( buffer );
```

which constructs a new instance of **mstring** from the string extracted from the input stream.

The third constructor function has an argument which is an mstring reference. It is a copy constructor that initialises a new **mstring** from an existing **mstring**. It is used in the program *teststring* in the statement

```
mstring c = b;
```

to make a new instance, mstring **c**, which is initialised from mstring **b**.

8.3.2 A further look at the second constructor function definition

This creates an **mstring** from a string as defined in the **string** library so functions can be used from this library. *strlen( )* is used to initialise the **len** data member.

The constructor ensures that the char array **p** data member does not become too large for the allocated storage. If the initialising string is too large then the constructor passes control to the private member function *error( )* which gives a message before terminating a program.

The components of **p** are initialised from the characters in the string excluding the null terminator.

8.3.3 A further look at the third constructor function definition

This initialises a new **mstring** from an existing **mstring** so the definition of this copy constructor must deal with two **mstring** objects and must therefore distinguish between them.

The data members of the new class object are accessed through their identifiers **len** and **p**. This new object is implicitly returned by the constructor.

The data members of the existing object **s**, which is the initialiser and the argument passed to the constructor, are accessed using the selection operators. Here they are accessed by direct selection using **s.len** and **s.p**.

```
mstring :: mstring( const mstring& s )
{
   len = s.len;
   for ( int i = 0; i <  len  ; i++ )
     p[ i ] = s.p[ i ];
}
```

8.4 Operator overloading

In most programming languages, operators can have only the definitions that are given within the compiler. In C++, however, users are allowed to define the action of most of the operator symbols when one or more operand is to be a class object. A new operator symbol definition is written as a modified function definition. The modification is made in the header line of the operator symbol definition by making the function identifier include the keyword **operator** followed by the symbol.

Programming in C++

As with overloaded function identifiers, the compiler distinguishes between the definitions for an operator symbol by consideration of the number and the types (or classes) of the operands.

All of the operator symbols listed in Appendix 2 can be overloaded, except for . and .* and :: and the conditional operator ? :. Each operator symbol retains its order of precedence, associativity and number of operands with the new definition.

With the exception of the assignment operator, all overloaded operator functions for class X are inherited by classes derived from X.

A function that defines the action of an overloaded operator may either be a member function or a friend function of the class declaring the type of one or more of the operands. There is no rule[1] to decide of which form the function should be, but a sensible convention often used is:

◇ an operator that has no side-effects (does not change its operands) is best declared as a friend, and

◇ an operator with side-effects on its first (or only) operand is best declared as a member of the class of that operand, if possible.

For both unary and binary operators, a friend operator overloading function needs one more argument than a member function performing the same action.

8.4.1 An example of a friend operator overloading function

The redefined equality comparison operator is used in the **if** statement in *teststring* in the boolean expression

```
( a == c )
```

It is used to see if the two **mstrings a** and **c** are the same. Whenever the operator is used, the two operands are unchanged so the definition is made to be a friend function within the class definition. Both the operands become arguments passed by value, and the members of the operand objects are accessed using selector operators. The function returns an integer (boolean) value.

```
int operator ==  ( const mstring s, const mstring t )
{
    if ( s.len != t.len ) return 0;
                        // return FALSE if lengths differ
    for ( int i = 0; i < s.len ; i++ )
        if ( s.p[ i ] != t.p[ i ] ) return 0;
            // return FALSE if corresponding chars differ
    return 1;    // return TRUE if lengths and chars same
}
```

---

[1]Except that the assignment operator =, subscript operator [], function call operator ( ), and the member selection . and -> operators are required to be class member functions.

8.4.2 An example of a member operator overloading function

The redefined compound assignment operator $+=$ symbol is used in the following statement in *teststring*:

```
response += a;
```

It is used to append a copy of the mstring **a** onto the end of mstring **response** (concatenation). The operand **response** is changed, but the operand **a** is unchanged. The function is defined as a member function of **mstring**.

The first operand, **response**, is the object to which the operator is applied, and its data members, **len** and **p**, are accessed directly.

The second operand, **a**, becomes the argument passed by value, and its data members are accessed using a selection operator.

All assignment operators return a reference for the assigned operand. In this case, the function needs to return a reference for **response**. A pointer to an object to which an overloaded operator definition is applied is given by the keyword **this**[2]. This pointer can be dereferenced, so ***this** is a reference for the operand. The definition for the compound assignment operator can be written as:

```
mstring& mstring :: operator +=  ( const mstring s )
{
   if (( len + s.len ) > LEN_MAX )
     error( );
   for ( int i = 0; i < s.len; i++ )
     p[ len + i ] = s. p[ i ];
                // copying components of b onto end of a
   len += s. len;           // adding lengths together
   return *this;                   /* returns reference
             to this mstring object being appended */
}
```

The following further points arise from this example definition.

In the statement

```
len += s.len;
```

the compiler will use its definition for the operator symbol $+=$ since the operands are **integers**. In fact, the operator symbol $+=$ is overloaded within the compiler since it holds definitions for the symbol with operands all of the predefined types.

A simple assignment operator symbol definition would be very similar to that for a copy constructor.

Finally, this definition ensures that concatenation does not allow the storage of one **mstring** object to overwrite the storage of another. If this would happen, then the program is abruptly terminated.

---

[2]**this** can be used in any member function. It is a pointer whose referenced type is the class in which the member function is defined.

8.4.3 Example of an overloaded extraction operator >>

The operator is used twice in *teststring*: it is used in the two statements
```
cin >> a;
cin >> b;
```
In both cases it is used to extract **mstring** objects from the input stream **cin**. The two operands, in each case, are a reference for an input stream and for an **mstring** object. Since the first operand is a member of the **istream** class, we make this function just a friend of the **mstring** class.

Because it is a friend function, both of the operands are passed as arguments to the function. Both of the operands are arguments passed by reference: we access and change both of the operands.

The extraction operator returns a reference for the current position in the input stream: a reference for the next item to be read. In the following definition, **is**, a formal argument, is the reference for the input stream. It is replaced by the actual argument **cin** when the operator is used in the program module.
```
istream& operator >> ( istream& is, mstring& s )
{
    char buffer[ LEN_MAX ];
    is. getline( buffer, LEN_MAX, '\n' );
    // reads up to 80 chars into buffer or up to newline
    s = mstring( buffer );
        // type conversion, using the second  constructor
    return is;        // returns reference to input stream
}
```
Within the C++ compiler are definitions of the extraction operator for each of the predefined types, so that **chars** and **integers** and **doubles** are extracted correctly from an input stream using the appropriate definition. This definition enables **mstrings** to be as easily read in.

8.4.4 Example of an overloaded insertion operator <<

This operator is used several times in *teststring* in statements such as
```
cout << message;
```
It is used to insert **mstring** objects into an output stream.

For the new definition of the operator two operands are needed, one of which is a reference for a position in an output **ostream** stream, and the other is an **mstring** object. The **mstring** object is unchanged, and a copy of it can be used, so the corresponding argument can be passed by value.

The characters held in the **mstring** data member **p** are inserted, in turn, using the definition for the insertion of chars held within the compiler.

An insertion operator definition returns the value of a reference for the insertion stream, giving the position for the next item to be written.

```
ostream& operator<< ( ostream& os, const mstring s )
{
  for ( int i = 0; i <= s. len ; i++ )
    os << s.p[i];
  return os;     // returns reference for output stream
}
```

Obviously, there are several definitions already for the insertion operator symbol, we are just giving another one.

8.5 Operator symbol definitions

From the examples in this chapter, we can see that function definitions and operator symbol definitions are almost identical in their format. The operands of an operator symbol can be considered to be similar to arguments of a function.

We often use an operator symbol, such as +, without thinking of the actions that must be performed to carry it out. We assume that the operator symbol + will add two integers and produce an integer result, or add two fractional, float, numbers and produce a float result. In fact, a computer handles integers and floats very differently, at its machine-level since **ints** are usually stored in two's complement form and **floats** are usually stored in IEEE single precision format. There must be different definitions (causing differing actions at run-time) for such an operator symbol with different types of operands. C++ allows us to provide further definitions, to be used by the compiler, for operator symbols when one or more operand is a class instance.

This is implemented using a modified form of a function definition, and because the compiler distinguishes between different function definitions by looking at the number and types of the arguments at a function call, operator overloading can be considered as just a special kind of function overloading.

8.6 Classes are user-defined types

In Chapter 2, introducing the predefined types, a *type* was said to determine the type(s) of the values that can be stored in an object, and defines the operations with which the object can be used in an expression.

We can now say exactly the same about a class: a *class* determines the type(s) of the values that can be stored in an object, and defines the operations with which the object can be used in an expression. For instance, an **mstring** has the stored values of its **len** and **p** (its data members), and **mstrings a** and **c** can be used in expression statements and expressions such as:

```
cin >> a;
response += a;
( a == c )
```

A class is also usually provided with constructor functions so that objects of that class can be declared and possibly initialised.

A class is also often provided with member and friend functions that can be used to handle objects of that class. These may be redefinitions of function identifiers already defined in libraries, and in base class definitions (also possibly stored in libraries).

So a class is a *user-defined type*. For the remaining chapters of this book, wherever the term *type* appears, it can be replaced by the term *type or class*.

A class whose definition is given in a library can also be considered to be an *abstract data type*. Such a type can be used to declare objects of that type, but the implementation details are hidden.

Most of the derived types that were considered in Chapter 4 can also be associated with classes: we can declare a pointer with a referenced class that can be used to hold the addresses of objects of that class, and we can declare arrays of class objects (all the components of the array must be of the same class). A struct is considered to be a particular form of a class: a class definition containing only public data members.

Exercises for Chapter 8

All of these exercises use program and library modules developed for the Exercises for Chapter 7.

1. Write the definition, in a header file, of a *tel_entry* class whose data members are *name* (up to 30 characters), and an unsigned integer *telephone_number*, which contains definitions for the extraction and insertion operators so that instances of the class can be read and written, and contains the definition of a relational operator so that the *name* of a *tel-entry* can be compared to see if it is 'greater' (in terms of its ASCII characters) than the *name* of another *tel_entry*.

2. Write the corresponding implementation file giving the full definitions for the (empty) constructor function for the *tel_entry* class and the definitions of the extraction, insertion and relational operators.

3. Write a program using the library developed in the first two Exercises that provides a user with a menu giving a choice of actions between entering up to ten *tel_entry* instances, reading entries from a file (both using the extraction operator definition), writing the instances to the screen and saving these in a data file (both using the insertion operator definition) and sorting them into aphabetical order by name (using the relational operator definition).

9 Dynamic memory allocation

So far, we have had to make requests for the maximum storage requirements for objects using their type or class definitions. This chapter shows how storage, of just the right size, can be allocated at run-time. These objects have *dynamic duration*; they can be allocated storage, and subsequently have the storage deallocated anywhere in a program.

An object's 'lifetime', that is, the period of time during program execution when storage is bound to the object, is referred to as an object's *duration* (5.7.3).

Objects declared with *file scope* (declared outside functions) have *static duration*. Storage is allocated by the compiler (often in a program's *data segment*) and remains bound to the object throughout program execution.

Objects declared within functions (including the main function) usually have *local scope* and then have *local duration*. Storage is allocated when a declaration is made, and at the end of the block in which an object is declared the storage is freed. Storage for such objects is usually given on a program's *run-time stack*.

We now consider how memory may be allocated at run-time from the *free store* to objects having *dynamic duration*. Every program is provided with a pool of unallocated memory that it may utilise during execution: this will be referred to here as the *free store*.

We allocate storage for an object with dynamic duration using the **new** operator, and we can release (deallocate) that storage using the **delete** operator. Allocation and subsequent deallocation requests, using these operators, may be made at any point in a program.

A feature of free store memory is that it cannot be *named*. Objects allocated space from the free store are manipulated indirectly through pointers.

Memory can be allocated dynamically to objects of any class, including those whose storage requirements are not known before run-time. Our arrays, so far, have had a length specified in their definition, and so have all been given this maximum storage even when it has not all been used. This chapter demonstrates how memory storage for an array can be allocated from the free store which is just the right size to hold that array.

Dynamic memory allocation of space from the free store is typically given to structures whose maximum extent is unknown before run-time, such as linked lists (stacks, queues, trees). This chapter first looks at simply linked lists, and develops class **node** and class **list** that can be used as base classes for any simply linked list.

As an example of a *homogeneous* linked list, class **myline** and class **mypage** are derived from class **node** and class **list**. These definitions are then used in a program that behaves like a primitive line-editor (of the sort used in the early 1970s) which reads in a text file and enables the inserting and deleting of lines from the file using line numbers, after which the edited file is then saved.

Objects linked in an *homogeneous linked list* are all instances of the same class.

In the final chapter, class **node** and class **list** are only slightly varied to provide base classes for an example program illustrating a *heterogeneous* linked list that links objects of differing classes.

9.1 Simply linked lists

Linked data structures are formed by making objects contain pointers to other objects. The pointers link the separate objects into a single data structure. The objects so linked are often called *nodes* and the node pointers can be data members of these node objects if the nodes are instances of a class.

A linked data structure can be neatly set up using two class definitions: one class, **list**, defining the overall linking structure, and a class definition for primitive nodes, class **node**.

The simplest linked structure is the *simply linked list*, where each node except the last contains a pointer to the next node in the list. A pointer *head* points to the first node in the list. The last node contains a *null* pointer with **int** value 0.

The diagram below illustrates a simply linked list of data objects where each object is held in a node:

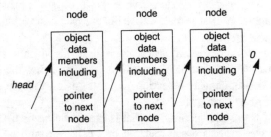

We can give the identifier *next* to the pointer indicating the next node in the list. This will be defined as a data member of class **node**.

We also need to consider the *current* pointer indicating the current node being handled, and the *previous* pointer which points to the node in which *current* is stored. These pointers, which give the relationship between the objects in the list structure, will be defined as data members of class **list**.

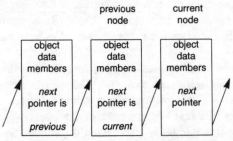

Diagram showing pointers and their relationship to the current node

9.2 Defining base classes for a simply linked list

We start by defining two classes that can form the base classes for a simply linked list. A class **list** object is a linked list of class **node** objects. The list will grow when nodes are added to the list and contract when nodes are deleted. Nodes can be added to the list at any time after the list has been declared, and can subsequently be deleted at any time. The nodes have dynamic duration.

Class **node** has only a single member, the data member **next** which is a pointer with the **node** referenced type; but class **list** will be *a friend class so that all members of class list have full access to the class node definition.*

The class **list** definition is also simple. The data members of the class are three pointers, all with the **node** referenced type: **head, previous,** and **current.** The member functions of class **list** enable us to construct an empty list, insert a new node before the current node, remove the current node, make the head node become the current node, and return a pointer to the next node.

9.2.1 The header file for class node and class list

```
// file list.h

class node
{
  private:
    node* next;                    // a pointer to nodes
  friend class list;
            // members of list have full access to node
};

class list
{
  private:
    node* head;
    node* previous;
    node* current;
  public:
    list( );                   // constructs an empty list
    void insert( node* );
                        // inserts a node into a list
    node* remove( );
            // returns a pointer to the removed node
    node* first( );
                // returns a pointer to the first node
    node* next( );
                // returns a pointer to the next node
};
```

9.2.2 Implementing the member functions for class list

The constructor function *list( )* is a simple one: it just initialises all the data members to the null pointer value, 0, to construct an empty list object. This implies that we must use *insert( )* to make the list grow before any other list handling is performed.

For most of the other functions, we need to access the **next** data members of the nodes. This access can be made using the indirect selection operator. So

```
    previous -> next
```
selects the pointer to the current node, **current**, and

```
    current -> next
```
selects the pointer to the node following the current node.

The *insert( )* function has an argument, **p**, that is a pointer to the node to be inserted. The function inserts this node before the current node. If the list is empty, then the new node will be inserted at the head of the list. Otherwise, the node is inserted between the previous node and the current node by assigning to **previous - > next** the value of **p**. The new node will now be the previous node to the current node, so **p - > next** is assigned the value of **current** and **previous** is now assigned the value of **p**. So the function can be:

```
void list :: insert ( node* p )
{
    if ( previous == 0 )
            head = p;
    else    previous -> next = p;
    p -> next = current;
    previous = p;
}
```

The *remove( )* function removes the current node and returns a pointer to this node (so that its storage can then be deallocated). If the list is empty, then null is returned. If the current node is the head node, then it can be removed by assigning to **head** the value of **current - > next**. Otherwise, the current node can be removed from the list by making **previous - > next** be **current - > next**. Finally, we need to declare a pointer to this current node that is being removed, alter the value in **current** so that it now points to the following node, and then return the pointer to the removed node. It can be written as:

```
node* list :: remove ( )
{
    if ( current == 0 ) return 0;
    if ( previous == 0 )
            head = current -> next;
    else    previous -> next = current -> next;
    node* p = current;
    current = current -> next;
    return p;
}
```
The remaining functions are straightforward.

9.2.3 *The implementation file*

```
// file list, the implementation file for list.h
#include <iostream.h>
#include "list.h"

list :: list( )
{
   head = previous = current = 0;
}

void list :: insert( node* p )
{
   if ( previous == 0 )
         head = p;
   else    previous -> next = p;
   p -> next = current;
   previous = p;
}

node* list :: remove( )
{
   if ( current == 0 ) return 0;
   if ( previous == 0 )
         head = current -> next;
   else    previous -> next = current -> next;
   node* p = current;
   current = current -> next;
   return p;
}

node* list :: first( )
{
   previous = 0;
   current = head;
   return current;
}

node* list :: next( )
{
   if ( current == 0 )
     return 0;
   previous = current;
   current = current -> next;
   return current;
}
```

9.3 Implementing an actual linked list structure

The classes **node** and **list** set up the essential structure and handling features needed to implement an actual linked list. Each of these classes can be used as a base class.

To illustrate an actual linked list which can grow and contract at run-time, the example program in this chapter is a simple line-editor for a page of no fixed length. With an editor (or word-processor) we expect to be able to use a text file (initially possibly empty), and to be able to insert lines and remove lines in any order. The program makes use of a library where lines are derived from **nodes** and the page is derived from class **list**.

A line will be an instance of class **myline** with the addition of a **next** pointer data member inherited from class **node**. Since we do not know how long each line to be inserted will be, the data members of class **myline** are **length** and a pointer with the **char** referenced type that will point to a storage area in the free store where the array of characters that will hold the line will be held. We will need to provide a definition of the subscript operator so that the pointer is correctly associated with the contents of this storage.

The page will be an instance of class **mypage**, and is just a simply linked list of **mylines**. However, because **next** was a **private** member of class **node**, it cannot be directly accessed by the member functions of class **mypage**, and so type conversions must be made within the functions of class **list** so that the member functions of class **mypage** can refer to pointers with the **myline** referenced type.

Before we consider the definitions of class **mypage** and class **myline** in more depth, we need to consider how free store can be allocated and deallocated to objects with dynamic duration.

9.4 Allocating and deallocating free store: the new and delete operators[1]

Space in the free store can be obtained by using the operator **new**. This operator returns a pointer to the beginning of the allocated space or returns null, 0, if no space in the free store is available.

Space in the free store can be deallocated by using the operator **delete** together with the value of the pointer that was returned when the space was originally allocated using **new**.

---

[1] The operators **new** and **delete** may be overloaded to provide alternative storage management, but this should be done with great care, particularly when a class hierarchy is involved. Such new definitions may not be virtual functions.

9.4.1 Using the new operator

To allocate free store memory for data objects we apply the operator **new** to a type or class specifier. Either a single object, or an array of objects can be allocated storage. The operator returns a pointer to the beginning of an amount of storage sufficent to hold an object of that class or type. This pointer is then assigned to a pointer of the given reference type. For example:

```
int*  p  = new int;
```

allocates memory to one object of type int, *p* is now a pointer to that storage, and

```
int* q = new int[ 150 ];
```

which allocates memory to an array with 150 integer components, *q* is a pointer to the first component (the array identifier), and

```
mask*  r = new mask( word )
```

which allocates memory to a *mask* class object, *r* is a pointer to the object; a class constructor then initialises that memory.

9.4.2 Using the delete operator

When an object with dynamic duration is no longer needed, the space it occupies should be released so that the memory is then available for others. The memory is deallocated by the **delete** operator. For all objects except arrays, the memory is deallocated by passing the pointer to the object, **p**, to the operator as in:

```
delete ( p );
```

If **p** is the null pointer, no action is taken; otherwise, memory is deallocated. If **p** is a pointer to a class object for which a destructor is defined, then the destructor will be called before the object is destroyed.

A complication arises if the data object to be destroyed is an array. If the components of the array are class objects for which a destructor is defined, the destructor must be called for each component of the array before the array, itself, can be destroyed. In this case, therefore, the **delete** operator needs to know the number of components in the array so that it will know how many times it must call the destructor. On the other hand, if the components of an array are not class objects, or if they are class objects for which no destructor has been defined, no destructors need to be called, and so the number of components is not required.

During the evolution of C++, three distinct methods for destroying arrays, to overcome this complication, have been introduced into the language. Only the latest method to appear is given here: an empty pair of square brackets is placed after the keyword **delete** to notify the operator that the object to be destroyed is an array. So the array pointed to by **p** is deallocated with the statement:

```
delete[ ] p;
```

An array often has components of a predefined type and is usually one of several data members of a class instance. It can be deallocated together with the rest of the storage for the object using **delete(p)**, where **p** is a pointer to that object.

9.5 Defining a class with a constructor using the free store

The lines needed for the page editing program may be of any length up to the maximum line-length that can be input. They can be defined as instances of the class **myline**; the full definition of this class is given in the *page* library files shown in 9.7.

The array holding the line characters is not given as a data member of the class but suffcent storage to hold a line is allocated from the free store by the constructor. So each line will be constructed with a different amount of storage allocated to it. The constructor of the class **myline** will need to have the string, holding the characters in the line, passed to it as an argument.

The data members of class **myline** are an integer **length** and a pointer **str** with the **char** referenced type, and the inherited member **next** (which is private to class node). The pointer **str** is not defined as the identifier of an array, and so we must provide a definition of the subscript operator **[ ]** so that **str** can be handled as an array identifier and used with subscripts to access a component.

Class **myline** is derived from class **node**. We need to provide definitions of the extraction and insertion operators so that mylines can be read and written. So the class definition can be written as:

```
class myline : private node
{
    private:
        int len;
        char* str;
    public:
        myline( const char* );
        char& operator[ ] ( int i ) { return str[ i ]; }
    friend istream& operator>> ( istream&, myline& );
    friend ostream& operator<< ( ostream&, const myline );
};
```

The definition for the subscript operator is given inline. It takes an integer argument and returns the corresponding component of the **char** free store allocation.

The constructor for an instance of a **myline** must find the length of the string passed to it and then use the **new** operator to obtain space in the free store for a **char** array of that length. The pointer returned by **new** is assigned to the pointer data member **str**. The components of this array must be initialised by the characters in the string. So the constructor can be written as:

```
myline :: myline( const char* s )
{ len = strlen( s );
    str = new char[ len ];
    for ( int i = 0; i <  len ; i++ )
        str[ i ] = s[ i ];
}
```

The definitions for the insertion and extraction operators are similar to those given in 8.1.2 for **mstrings**.

9.6 Explicitly converting pointer referenced types

The class **mypage** is derived from class **list.** It inherits the member functions of this class, but these functions use the pointer referenced type of **node,** and we want our class **mypage** to insert and remove **mylines.** The pointer **next** is also **private** to class **node** and, since class **mypage** is not given as a friend class of this class, cannot handle it directly.

The definition of class **mypage** should be similar to that of class **list** but with pointers of different referenced types:

```
class mypage : private list
{
   public:
      void insert_line( myline* p );
      myline* remove_line( );
      myline* first_line( );
      myline* next_line( );
};
```

There is no need for a constructor function for class **mypage** since a suitable constructor function is inherited from class **list** (a constructor of an empty list).

Consider the member function *insert_line( )* which inserts a **myline** into a **mypage.** This can be built from the *insert( )* function whose class scope is that of class **list,** but the pointer to the **myline,** given by the identifier **p,** say, must be converted into a pointer of the **node** referenced type before it is passed to that function. We can use the type cast operator, (*type*), to convert the referenced type of **p** with the expression (**node***) **p.** So the **mypage** *insert( )* member function definition is:

```
void mypage :: insert_line( myline* p )
{
   list :: insert( ( node* ) p );
}
```

The other member functions of class **mypage** all return pointers with the **myline** referenced type. Again, they can be built from the corresponding member functions of class **list,** but for these functions it is the return value that must be converted to type **myline*** before it is returned using the type cast operator with the form (**myline***). The *remove( )* function is then:

```
myline* mypage :: remove_line( )
{
   return ( myline* )( list :: remove( ) );
}
```

The remaining member functions are defined in a similar way.

9.7 The library files defining an actual simply linked structure

The full definitions for class **myline** and class **mypage** can now be put into a
header and corresponding implementation file.

9.7.1 The header file for the actual linked structure

```
// file page.h
#include "list.h"
const MAX_LINE = 80;

class myline : private node
{
   private:
      int len;
      char* str;
   public:
      myline( const char* );
      char& operator[ ] ( int i ) { return str[ i ]; }
   friend istream& operator>> ( istream&, myline& );
   friend ostream& operator<< ( ostream&, const myline );
};

class mypage : private list
{
   public:
      void insert_line( myline* p );
      myline* remove_line( );
      myline* first_line( );
      myline* next_line( );
};
```

9.7.2 The implementation file for the actual linked structure

```
// file page, the implementation file for page.h
#include <iostream.h>
#include <string.h>
#include "page.h"

// constructor for mylines
myline :: myline( const char* s )
{
   len = strlen( s );
   str = new char[ len ];
   for ( int i = 0; i <  len ; i++ )
      str[ i ] = s[ i ];
}
```

```
// definition of extraction operator for mylines
istream& operator>> ( istream& is, myline& t )
{
    char buffer[ MAX_LINE ];
    is.getline( buffer, MAX_LINE, '\n' );
    t = myline( buffer );
    return is;
}

// definition of insertion operator for mylines
ostream& operator<< ( ostream& os, const myline t )
{
    for ( int i = 0; i < t.len ; i++ )
        os << t.str[i];
    return os;
}

// definitions of mypage member functions
void mypage :: insert_line( myline* p )
{
    list :: insert( ( node* )p );
}

myline* mypage :: remove_line( )
{
    return ( myline* )( list :: remove( ) );
}

myline* mypage :: first_line( )
{
    return ( myline* )( list :: first( ) );
}

myline* mypage :: next_line( )
{
    return ( myline* )( list :: next( ) );
}
```

9.8 A program example using the actual linked list definition

This program shows objects with static duration: **page** and **p**; all functions within
the program can use them and their duration is for all the time for which the
program is run (they have file scope). The storage allocated to **page** holds the
values of **head**, **previous**, and **current** (data members inherited from class **list**).

There are also a number of objects with local duration such as **command**,
n and **i** (they have local scope). They are probably each given space on a stack
every time they are declared and this is deallocated when the end of the block,
in which they are declared, is reached.

There are also objects with dynamic duration. Some of these are the lines read in from the input file. The storage space is allocated using **new** and then the *insert_line( )* member function of **mypage** is used to link the objects into the list. Further objects are similarly allocated space and inserted into the linked list when the function *i( )*, defined in the program file, is used to input new lines from the keyboard. The exceptional possibility that there may be no free store available is discussed in Chapter 11.

Objects in the list are deallocated storage space when the user deletes them using the *d( )* function, defined in the program, and finally, at the end of program execution, when the objects remaining in the list are stored into the output file.

The command line for this program, when it is run, is of the form:

```
edit_page   text1   text2
```

where **text1** is an input file that may already contain text, and **text2** holds the output with the alterations made to the text.

```
// file edit_page
#include <iostream.h>
#include <fstream.h>
#include "page.h"

void i( );
void d( );
void w( );


mypage page;
myline* p;

void main( int argc, char* argv[ ] )
{
   char command, line[ MAX_LINE ];
   ifstream infile;
   infile.open( argv[ 1 ], ios :: in);
   while ( !infile.eof( ) )
     {
       infile.getline( line, MAX_LINE, '\n' );
       p = new myline( line );
       page.insert_line( p );
     }
   infile.close( );

   do
     {
       cout << "Give a command of: " << endl
            << "i for inserting a line" << endl
            << "d for deleting a line" << endl
            << "w for writing all lines" << endl
            << "q to quit" << endl
            << "Command given is: ";
       cin >> command;
```

```
        switch (command)
          {
            case 'i': i( ); break;
            case 'd': d( ); break;
            case 'w': w( ); break;
            case 'q': break;
            default: cout << "\nIncorrect letter"
                          << "Try again." << endl;
          }
       } while (command != 'q' );

    ofstream outfile;
    outfile.open( argv[ 2 ], ios::out );
    for (p=page.first_line( ); p!=0; p=page.next_line( ))
        outfile << *p << endl;
    outfile.close( );
}

void i( )
{
    myline* q;   char line[ MAX_LINE ]; int n;
    cout << "\nGive number of line before insertion,\n"
         << " then enter line you wish to insert:" << endl;
    cin >> n;
    cin.getline( line, MAX_LINE, '\n' );
    q = new myline( line );
    p = page.first_line( );
    for ( int i = 1; i < n; i++ )
      p = page.next_line( );
    page.insert_line( q );

}

void d( )
{
    int n;
    cout << "\nGive number of line you wish to delete: ";
    cin >> n;
    p = page.first_line( );
    for ( int i = 1; i < n; i++ )
      p = page.next_line( );
    page.remove_line( );
    delete( p );
}

void w( )
{
    int i = 1;
    for (p=page.first_line();p!=0;p=page.next_line(),i++)
      cout << i << *p << endl;
}
```

Exercises for Chapter 9

1. Write suitable class definitions, in a header file, for an actual simply linked list structure with nodes that are *tel_entry* instances. A *tel-entry* should have data members of *name* (up to LINE_LENGTH characters), and an unsigned *telephone_number*, and should be provided with member functions for extraction and insertion.

2. Write the corresponding implementation file giving full definitions for all the member functions declared in the header file written for Exercise 1.

3. Develop a program that uses the library created in Exercises 1 and 2 to provide the user with a menu giving a choice of actions including reading telephone details from a file, entering new a set of details, removing a set of details, saving the details in a file.

4. Extend the library and program developed in the previous exercises so that a user can sort telephone details into alphabetic order by *name*.

5. Develop a linked list structure definition that performs like a stack; a stack is a last-in-first-out list where items can only be added to the head of the stack and removed from the head of the stack. Write a program that tests this definition.

6. Develop a linked list struuucture definition that performs like a queue; a queue is a first-in-first-out list where items can only be added to the tail of the queue and removed from the head of the queue. It may be useful to have node pointers to previous nodes as well as to the next nodes. Write a program that tests this definition.

10 Templates

C++ is, in many respects, a strongly-typed language. In particular, as we have seen, a C++ compiler chooses which function definition to bind to the code from consideration of the actual argument types and classes associated with a call when an overloaded function identifier is used. This means that a separate definition is required for all the possible argument types[1] that a program may require to be associated with that function identifier.

A program may also require several similar class definitions to provide sets of objects that differ only in member types.

The writing of such multiple definitions is tedious, but fortunately a C++ compiler can be made to generate them. C++ provides the programmer with the ability to write a function or a class definition with non-specific, *generic*, argument types: a **function template** or a **class template**. Declarations of such functions or objects of such classes, with specific argument types, causes the compiler to generate an actual *instantiation* with the given types.

This is obviously a helpful feature of the language. However, the full potential of the help this feature can provide has not yet been realised in the C++ version which this book discusses. This chapter concludes with some reservations about the implementation of templates in this C++ version.

This chapter also shows how class data members can be initialised using a constructor initialisation list.

10.1 The template formal type parameter list

In a template, the generic types are themselves *parameters* (arguments) of the template. They are given in a *formal type parameter list*, which is a comma-separated list between angle brackets, after the keyword **template** introducing the template definition.

The formal type parameter list cannot be empty. The formal types that it contains are replaced with actual types by the compiler throughout the following template definition whenever the compiler generates an instantiation of a template.

Each formal type parameter which represents a generic type consists of the keyword **class** followed by the formal type parameter identifier. Each identifier can occur only once in the formal type parameter list.

The formal type parameter list can also contain specific type parameters. These are represented by the type identifier followed by the parameter identifier.

---

[1]A class is usually a user-defined type. For the rest of this chapter, wherever the term *type* is used it can be replaced throughout by *type or class*.

Examples of formal type parameter lists following the template keyword

```
template < class T >  // one generic type, identifier T
template < class T, class U, char c >
                // two generic types and one specific type
```

10.2 Function templates

These enable us to write a function definition for a function identifier with generic argument types. The function template, in itself, does not define anything. However, when a template function declaration is made, using *specific argument types*, the compiler will generate an actual function definition providing the actual definition uses definitions for operators and functions that are known to it, and there is no other definition provided for these specific argument types.

Careful consideration needs to be given to the operands of operators and arguments of functions within a **template** definition to ensure that definitions exist and that those that do exist carry out the action required when the generic types are replaced by specific types. If necessary, an alternative definition to that of a **template** instantiation must be provided. Such an alternative definition will be used by the compiler, *overriding* the generation of a template function.

The return-type of a function template need not be a formal type parameter even though this is the case in the example program shown in 10.2.2.

A function template may be given for a set of inline functions and, in this case, the keyword **inline** preceeds the function return-type in the usual way.

10.2.1 Function templates and function definitions

The program example shown below illustrates the form of a function template definition. The program contains a function template for a set of functions whose task is to return the larger of two objects where both are of the type or class **T**:

```
template < class T >
T max( T x, T y )
{
    return ( ( x > y ) ? x : y );
}
```

It would seem reasonably useful to generate a set of such functions to add to the functions provided to handle objects of various types. Its usefulness becomes more apparent when a key feature of template generation is appreciated: *a formal type parameter can only be replaced exactly by a type or class*. No implicit conversions are permitted.

The relational operator, $>$, is defined for operands of all the predefined types, but the expression (x $>$ y) is evaluated using, if necessary, implicit type conversion through promotion, so it can be used to compare a **char** with an **int** or a **float**. Stricter comparisons may be required.

The program declares two template function prototypes:

```
int max( int, int );
char max( char, char );
```

The first declaration causes the generation of a function where **T** is replaced by **int**, and only two **int**egers can be compared. The second declaration causes the generation of a function where **T** is replaced by **char** and only two **char**acters can be compared. If the program is run and a data item entered which is not of the requested type then the corresponding *max( )* for that type will not execute.

The program also contains a definition for **max(char*, char*)** which the compiler uses instead of generating a definition from the template function. When the compiler meets a function prototype it first searches to see if a function definition with the same function identifier and same signature exists in the program files or included library files. If such a definition is found then it will be used and be bound to the code at the appropriate points. If such a definition is not found, the compiler looks for a template for the function definition, and uses the template to generate a definition if the template exists.

The overriding function definition, with signature (**char***, **char***), has been given so that a sensible comparison can be made between strings. If a template function with this signature was generated, then the expression (**x** > **y**) would compare a pointer to a pointer, which is unlikely to be the task required of this function.

Although this example program only requires the generation of functions from the template function using predefined types as the specific replacement types, functions could be generated by replacing **T** with a *class_identifier* (provided, of course, that the operator symbol > is defined by a member or friend function of *class_identifier*).

10.2.2 Program example showing a function template

```
// file compare

#include <iostream.h>
#include <string.h>

/* template function declarations, causing generation of
                                    function definitions */
int max( int, int );
char max( char, char );

//   normal function declarations
char* max( char*, char* );
void max_int( );
void max_char( );
void max_string( );
```

```
void main( )
{
   do
    {
      cout << "Commands are"              << endl
           << "I to compare two integers" << endl
           << "C to compare two chars"  << endl
           << "S to compare two strings" << endl
           << "Q to quit. Enter command: ";

      char command;
      cin >> command; cin.ignore( 80, '\n' );

      switch ( command )
        {
           case 'I': max_int( ); break;
           case 'C': max_char( ); break;
           case 'S': max_string( ); break;
        }
    } while ( command != 'Q' );
}

template < class T >    // function template definition
T max( T x, T y )
{
   return ( ( x > y ) ? x : y );
}

char* max( char* s1, char* s2 )// overriding definition
{
   return ( ( strlen( s1 ) >  strlen( s2 ) ) ? s1 : s2 );
}

void max_int( )                // uses a template function
{
   int i1, i2;
   cout << "Enter two integers: ";
   cin >> i1; cin >> i2;
   cout << "Largest is: " << max( i1, i2 ) << endl;
}

void max_char( )               // uses a template function
{
   char c1, c2;
   cout << "Enter two chars: ";
   cin >> c1; cin >> c2;
   cout << "Largest is: " << max( c1, c2 ) << endl;
}
```

```
void max_string( )        // uses the overriding definition
{
   char s1[ 20 ], s2[ 20 ];
   cout << "Enter two words: ";
   cin >> s1; cin >> s2;
   cout << "Largest is: " << max( s1, s2 ) << endl;
}
```

10.3 Constructor initialisation lists

For the example programs illustrating class templates in the next sections, the class constructors use an argument, passed to the constructor when a class object is declared, to initialise a data member. The argument is assigned unchanged to the data member.

For such simple initialisations, a *constructor initialisation list* can be used to assign arguments directly to data members. For example, suppose a class of rectangles is defined with data members *length* and *breadth* in a definition:

```
class rectangle
{
   private:
     int length;
     int breadth;
   public:
     rectangle( int, int );                  // constructor
        . . .
};
```

Suppose that the constructor just uses its two arguments to initialise the data members, so it could be written:

```
rectangle :: rectangle( int i, int j )
{
   length = i;
   breadth = j;
}
```

In this case, since data members are assigned arguments directly, the constructor could also be written, using an initialisation list, as:

```
rectangle :: rectangle( int i, int j )
                     : length( i ), breadth( j ) {  }
```

The constructor initialisation list is separated by a colon from the constructor argument list, and the arguments used for assignment are passed to the data members in parentheses as shown (in the same way that derived class constructors use a base class constructor initialisation list, introduced in 7.4.2).

If a constructor has multiple arguments, and possibly uses such an initialisation list, then declaration initialisation cannot be performed with a simple assignment. A declaration and initialisation of a rectangle instance, **r**, using the constructor shown, would then be made by the following statement, say,:

```
rectangle r( 3, 4 );
```

10.4 Class templates with generic parameters

We first consider class templates where the formal type parameter lists only contain generic types.

The example program given in 10.4.2 shows a class template for **myarray**s. These myarrays can have components of any type, and can be of any length required by the user of the program. The type of the components is given by the generic type **T** in the class template definition.

The type and length of a specific **myarray** is given in its declaration. The program shows two such declarations and initialisations, where the length (number of components) of a myarray, **size**, has been entered by the user. Since there is one argument given to the constructor, it can be given by a simple assignment:

```
myarray< int >   int_myarray = size;
                            // declaring an int array
myarray< char >  char_myarray = size;
                            // declaring a char array
```

In each of these declarations, the specific type of the myarray which replaces the generic type of the class template definition *is given between angle brackets after the class_identifier.*

For each of these declarations, the compiler generates and binds the class definition to the code and the size of each myarray is determined at run-time. The class definition, therefore, must be independent of the size of a myarray. So the myarray data members are a *pointer* and an integer to hold the size. These are both **private** members[2].

The pointer is used as an array identifier within the class constructor function and within a *write( )* function to display a **myarray**. The subscript operator **[ ]** needs to be defined so that the pointer can be used as an array identifier.

The subscript operator definition is given inline. The operator returns a T type reference.

---

[2]**private** by default in the definition, since no protection mode is specified.

The class template is therefore:

```
template < class T >
class myarray
{
    T*   a;                  // pointer of type (or class) T
    int len;                      // number of components
  public:
    myarray( int );                         // constructor
    T& operator[ ] ( int i ) { return a[ i ]; }
                         // subscript operator definition
    void write( );
};
```

The definitions of the other class template member functions which are not defined inline have a modified header line. They also start with the keyword **template** followed by the formal type parameter list for the class template, but the function identifier is also followed by the generic type identifiers in a comma-separated list held within angle brackets.

The *write( )* function, which writes out all the components of the array each separated by a space, has the full class template definition form for a member function of:

```
template < class T >
void myarray< T > :: write( )
{
   for ( int i = 0; i < len; i++ )
     cout << a[ i ] << ' ';
   cout << endl;
}
```

The constructor function uses a constructor initialisation list to assign the value of *size* (input by the user) to the data member **len**. It uses the operator **new** to allocate free store at run-time to an array of *size* components, each of the specific type given in the declaration.

```
template < class T >
myarray< T > :: myarray( int n ) : len( n )
{
   a = new T[ n ];
}
```

10.4.1 Program example of a class template with generic parameters

```
// file myarray1
#include <iostream.h>
```

```
// class template definition
template < class T >
class myarray
{
    T*  a;
    int len;
  public:
    myarray( int );
    T& operator[ ] ( int i ) { return a[ i ]; }
    void write( );
};

// class template constructor definition
template < class T >
myarray< T > :: myarray( int n ) : len( n )
{
  a = new T[ n ];
}

// class template member function definition
template < class T >
void myarray< T > :: write( )
{
  for ( int i = 0; i < len; i++ )
    cout << a[ i ] << ' ';
  cout << endl;
}

void main( )
{
  int size; char ch;

  cout << "Give size of integer array required: ";
  cin >> size;

  myarray< int >  int_myarray = size;
            // declaration of a template class object
  for ( int i = 0; i < size; i++ )
    int_myarray[ i ] = i;
            // integer array holds ascending integers
  int_myarray.write( );

  cout << "Give size of char array required: ";
  cin >> size;

  myarray< char >   char_myarray = size;
            // declaration of a template class object
  for ( ch = 'a', i = 0; i < size; i++, ch++ )
    char_myarray[ i ] = ch;
                  // char array holds ascending letters
  char_myarray.write( );
}
```

10.5 Class templates using constant expression parameters

The formal type parameter list of a class template can include constant expression parameters as well as generic types. The actual expressions given for such parameters must be constants and must be evaluated at compile-time.

The program example given in 10.5.1 shows such a mixed formal type parameter list in the class template definition:

```
template < class T, int n >
```

In such a list, the identifiers associated with the keyword **class** are formal generic type identifiers; other identifiers represent constant expressions of the given type.

These identifiers must then be given to class template member function definitions, as shown in the program example function definition header lines:

```
template < class T, int n >
myarray< T, n > :: myarray( ): len( n )
```
and
```
template < class T, int n >
void myarray< T, n > :: write( )
```

In this program example, as in the previous program example, **n** is used to initialise the length (*size*) of a **myarray** upon declaration. However, in this example, **n** is now a formal parameter of the class template and the actual replacement value must be known to the compiler so that a class definition can be generated. Moreover **n** must be replaced by a constant integer value.

So in this program example, both of the myarray classes generated have a length fixed within the program code. The **int_myarray** has six components since its declaration is given by:

```
     myarray< int, 6 >  int_myarray;
```
The length of the **char_myarray** is given by *size* in the template class declaration:
```
     myarray< char, size >  char_myarray;
```
but *size* must be **const**ant and its value known to the compiler.

10.5.1 Program using a class template with a constant expression parameter

```
// file myarray2
#include <iostream.h>
// class template definition
template < class T, int n >
class myarray
{
    T* a;
    int len;
  public:
    myarray( );
    T& operator[ ] ( int i ) { return a[ i ]; }
    void write( );
};
```

```
// constructor definition
template < class T, int n >
myarray< T, n > :: myarray( ): len( n )
                           // n is a constant expression
{
  a = new T[ n ];
}


// member function definition
template < class T, int n >
void myarray< T, n > :: write( )
{
  for ( int i = 0; i < len; i++ )
    cout << a[ i ] << ' ';
  cout << endl;
}


void main( )
{
  const int size = 4;
                  // myarray length cannot be variable
  char ch;

  myarray< int, 6 >  int_myarray;
                    // declaring an integer array
  for ( int i = 0; i < 6; i++ )
    int_myarray[ i ] = i;
  int_myarray.write( );

  myarray< char, size > char_myarray;
                        // declaring a char array
  for ( ch = 'a', i = 0; i < size; i++, ch++ )
    char_myarray[ i ] = ch;
  char_myarray.write( );
}
```

In this second example program illustrating class templates, the use of a constant expression parameter has considerably reduced the flexibility of array generation!

10.6 Reservations on the current templates definition

The programs in this chapter, developed to illustrate template definitions, all placed the template definitions within the program file. The compiler needs to see the full template definition (including those for template class member functions) to be able to generate an actual template function or template class instantiation within a file.

Care needs to be taken when it is preferred to have template definitions placed in libraries. If programs are to make instantiations, then template definitions must be given in a header file. If programs are not to make instantiations, then these must be made within the library implementation file where template definitions are held, and declarations for these instantiations must be provided in the library header file.

When a specific type replaces a generic type, no conversions or promotions can be made at any point within a definition, nor can a constant be replaced by a non-constant (or vice versa). Exact, and only exact, replacement is made. There is currently some debate about this restrictive rule which can lead to a multiplicity of definitions but, on the other hand, each definition has the virtue of being absolutely type-safe.

Finally, there still needs to be further work done within the C++ template syntax. Compilers make different assumptions about some parts of the syntax, and so template definitions may not be completely portable between implementations.

Exercises for Chapter 10

1. Write a function template for functions that compare the values of objects of the same type and return an integer value that indicates whether the values are equal or not.

Use the definition in a program to generate functions to compare the values of objects of the following types for equality:
   (i)   **integers,**
   (ii)   **chars,**
   (iii)   strings,
   (iv)   **mystrings** (as defined in Chapter 8).

2. Write a class template that can be used to generate classes whose instances are two-dimensional arrays with components of the pre-defined types. Provide for these classes overloading definitions for the extraction and insertion operators, so that instances can be read and written.

Use the definition in a program which declares two-dimensional arrays of **chars** and **integers**, reads values into these arrays, and writes them out when required.

3. Repeat Exercise 2, but use constant expression parameters within the class template to restrict the two-dimensional arrays to have only 3 * 5 components.

11 Virtual functions and virtual base classes

This chapter shows how the rules governing inheritance between a base class and derived classes are extended in C++ to enable the object-oriented programming concept of *polymorphism*. Languages implementing this concept permit objects of different classes to respond to a *message* in different ways.

In C++, such a message is a *virtual function call*. A virtual function, defined in a base class, can be redefined in derived classes so that objects of these derived classes will respond in different ways to what is, apparently, the same function call. A virtual function definition is bound to the program code, using a pointer, at run-time; this is known as *late binding* or *dynamic binding*.

An *abstract base class* definition holds one or more *pure virtual function* definitions. No objects of a abstract base class can be declared.

This chapter also shows how the use of a *virtual base class* can resolve a problem that may otherwise occur with multiple inheritance.

11.1 Selecting virtual functions

The keyword **virtual** is used in the prototype of a member function given within a base class definition. The virtual function definition can then be overridden by another definition in a derived class *that has the same identifier and signature*.

The overriding is accomplished in a program through the use of a pointer whose referenced type is that of the base class. If this pointer is then assigned the address of an object of a derived class, where the virtual function has been redefined, it can be used to indirectly select the derived class virtual function definition at run-time.

This contrasts to the indirect selection of an ordinary member function using such a pointer when, as would be expected, the base class definition corresponding to the function identifier and signature is selected.

Virtual function calls are implemented using a table of pointers to such function definitions. Although this is transparent to the user, it imposes a small run-time overhead.

11.2 Example program illustrating virtual functions

The program illustrates the difference in inherited behaviour between ordinary member functions and virtual member functions when they are indirectly selected with a base class pointer.

The program uses the *line* library in which a simple base class *crosses* is defined that includes a virtual function *write1( )* and an ordinary member function *write2( )*. The library also holds the definitions for two derived classes *stars*, and *queries* in which both *write1( )* and *write2( )* are redefined.

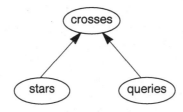

The inheritance diagram for the **crosses** family of classes

In the program file, objects of each of these classes are declared, together with a pointer **p** whose referenced class is *crosses*. This pointer is assigned, and reassigned, at run-time, to hold the address of a base class object or a derived class object. This pointer is used to indirectly select one of the virtual function *write1( )* definitions, at run-time, when the following statement is executed:

        p -> write1( );

If **p**, through the use of the switch default, holds the address of a base class *crosses* object **cross**, then the *write1( )* definition in the base class is used which writes out **cross** once.

If **p** is assigned the address of a derived class *stars* object **star**, then the *write1( )* definition in the *stars* class is used which writes out **star** twice.

If **p** is assigned the address of a derived class *queries* object **query**, then the *write1( )* definition in the *queries* class is used which writes out **query** three times.

These alternative actions performed on an object by the virtual function *write1( )* can be contrasted by the single action performed by the ordinary member function *write2( )* if the statement above is replaced by

        p -> write2( );

In all cases here, when the program is run, the definition for *write2( )* given in the base class is used which writes out a **cross**, **star**, or **query** object once depending on the last address assigned to **p**.

The indirect selection of a derived class ordinary member function redefinition of an inherited member function can only be achieved through a pointer whose referenced type is the derived class. For example, the *stars* definition of *write2( )* would be used if the declaration

        stars* q;

is made before the statement

        q -> write2( );

In this case, the compiler would bind the *stars* definition to the code.

11.2.1 The line library header file containing the class definitions

The keyword **virtual** is used to declare a virtual member function within the base class definition. It is not necessary to use the keyword within derived class definitions nor with a virtual function definition held within a library implementation file.

```
// file line.h

// base class definition including a virtual function

class crosses
{
  protected:
    char  p[ 6 ];      // data member can hold a string
  public:
    crosses( );                                   // constructor
             /* both of the following member functions
                    write the object pointed to once */
    virtual void write1( )
          { cout << p;  }    // virtual member function
    void write2( )
          { cout << p;  }    // ordinary member function
};

/* derived classes redefining virtual and ordinary
                                  member functions */
class stars : public crosses
{
  public:
    stars( );                                 // constructor
                /* both of these member functions
                  write the object pointed to twice */
    void write1( )
          { cout << p << p;  }
    void write2( )
          { cout << p << p;  }
};

class queries : public crosses
{
  public:
    queries( );                               // constructor
                    /* both of these member functions
              write the object pointed to three times */
    void write1( )
          { cout << p << p  << p;  }
    void write2( )
          { cout << p << p  << p;  }
};
```

11.2.2 The library implementation file

This just holds the constructor member function definitions for the three classes. The constructor functions for the derived classses are derived from the constructor function for the base class as discussed in 7.4.2.

```
// file line, implementation file for line.h
#include "line.h"

/* base class constructor constructs a string of four x
                    characters and a newline character */
crosses :: crosses( )
{
   for ( int i = 0; i < 4; i++ )
      p[ i ] = 'x';
   p[ 4 ] = '\n';
   p[ 5 ] = '\0';
}

// constructor for a class derived from the base class

stars :: stars( ) : crosses( )
{
   for ( int i = 0; i < 4; i++ )  p[ i ] = '*';
}

// constructor for a class derived from the base class

queries :: queries( ) : crosses( )
{
   for ( int i = 0; i < 4; i++ )  p[ i ] = '?';
}
```

11.2.3 The program file

This gives the user a choice of actions. However, all the commands lead to the execution of just one statement:

```
        p -> write1( );
```

The definition of the virtual function *write1( )* that is then bound to the program code depends on the class of the object whose address is stored in **p** at that time.

When the program is executed, if the command **2** is entered requesting 'triple queries', then the output is:

```
????
????
????
```

The command **0** (to quit) will cause the switch default case to assign the address of a *crosses* object **cross** to **p**, and so execution will end with the output:

xxxx

If this statement is changed by replacing the virtual function identifier with the ordinary member function identifier *write2( )*, then the definition associated with the referenced type of **p** is bound to the code by the compiler at translation time and so the object whose address is currently in **p** is written out just once whichever command is given.

```
// file virtfn

#include <iostream.h>
#include "line.h"

const LINE_LENGTH = 80;

void main( )
{
  int command;
// declaring objects of base class and derived classes
  crosses cross;
  stars star;
  queries query;
        // declaring a pointer to base class instances
  crosses* p;

  do
    {
        cout    << "Do you want to -"    << endl
                << "1 double stars"      << endl
                << "2 triple queries"    << endl
                << "0 quit."             << endl
                << "Enter command: ";
        cin >> command;  cin.ignore( LINE_LENGTH, '\n' );

        switch ( command )
          {
            case 1:  p = &star;  break;
            case 2:  p = &query;  break;
            default: p = &cross;
          }

        p -> write1( );
                            // selecting virtual function
    } while ( command != 0 );
}
```

In the terms of object-oriented programming, *write1( )* is a message. The response to the message depends on the class of the object to which it has been sent. The response is polymorphic: the form of the response differs between classes.

11.3 Pure virtual functions and abstract base classes

It may often happen that only derived classes objects may need to be declared. In this case, a virtual function may be given an empty definition in the base class, and each derived class will then give a full definition for the virtual function or inherit the empty definition. A virtual function with an empty definition may be declared within the class definition as, for example, **virtual void write( ) { }**

This is an alternative to giving the definition of a *pure virtual function* within a class definition as, for example,

```
virtual void write( )  =  0;
```

This form of declaration is allowed in current versions of C++, and a class which includes one or more pure virtual function declarations within the class definition is known as an *abstract base class*.

No objects of an abstract base class can be declared (though pointers with that class as a referenced class may be declared). The purpose of such a class is to provide an inheritance for classes which are derived from it, and enable objects of those classes to exhibit polymorphism through their class definitions for the inherited virtual functions.

11.4 Virtual base classes

In larger applications, where classes are derived from more than one base class, it may well be the case that a class inherits from a base class more than once via differing derivation pathways.

This is obviously the case within the **ios** family which includes the **iostream** class (as can be seen from the inheritance diagram given in Appendix 5). The **iostream** class inherits **ios** class definitions both from its **istream** inheritance and from its **ostream** inheritance. It would appear, for instance, that the **ios** constructor is invoked twice when an **iostream** object is declared. In fact this is not the case since **ios** is defined as a *virtual base class* in both the **istream** class definition and the **ostream** class definition. When a class inherits from a virtual base class through more than one derivation *only one set of definitions is inherited from the virtual base class*. The following example program shows how a virtual base class can be defined and used.

11.5 Example program handling a hierarchy of classes

The final example program of this book uses libraries that define a slight variation of the simply linked list given in 9.2, and a hierarchy of classes including an abstract base class and a virtual base class. The program itself gives the user the opportunity to insert instances of classes into the linked list (called a **page**) and to write out the page either to the screen or to a data file.

The linked list is a *heterogeneous* linked list since the nodes can be objects of different classes.

11.5.1 The library defining the simply linked list

This library holds modifications of the definition of the class **node** discussed in Chapter 9. The modifications only affect the header file of the library. The implementation file, defining the member functions of class **list**, is an exact copy of that given in 9.2.3.

The definition of class **node** is altered in two ways: the data member **next** is made **public**, and a pure virtual member function *write( )* is added.

The data member **next** is a pointer to **nodes**. By making it **public**, it becomes available as a pointer whose referenced type can be the base class for a hierarchy of classes. It can be used specifically within a program that includes the library. It can be used to select virtual function definitions from a hierarchy of classes whose base class is class **node**.

The pure virtual member function *write( )* is defined by

```
virtual void write( ostream& ) = 0;
```

The signature of this function is the single argument, an **ostream** reference. All the other definitions of this virtual function, within the hierarchy of class definitions, must have *the same signature*.

Because a pure virtual function is defined within the class **node** definition, this class is an abstract base class and no declarations of **node** instances can be made by a program including this library.

The header file of the library is:

```
// file virt_node.h

class node                          // an abstract base class
  {
  public:
    node* next;                     // a pointer to nodes
    virtual void write( ostream& ) = 0;
                    // a pure virtual member function
    friend class list;

  };

  class list                          // as in 9.2.1
  {
    node* head;
    node* previous;
    node* current;
  public:
    list( );
    void insert( node* p );
    node* remove( );
    node* first( );
    node* next( );
  };
```

11.5.2 The library header file defining the classes used by the program

This library provides the user with classes derived from **node** so that actual nodes can be declared and inserted into an instance of **list**. These classes are **text**, (instances store a line of characters), **divider** (instances store a line of hyphens), and **header** which is derived from both **text** and **divider** to provide instances for putting a given line of text into upper-case letters with a given indentation.

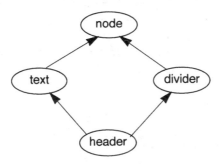

An inheritance diagram for the **node** family of classes

The definitions of both the **text** and **divider** classes inherit a **next** data member from the class **node** definition.

Since the **header** class definition inherits from both the **text** and **divider** class definitions, these both define **node** to be a **virtual** base class to ensure that the **header** definition inherits just one **next** data member, resolving any ambiguity.

```
// file page_node.h

#include "virt_node.h"

/* class constructor provides storage for an array of
                        characters from the free store */
class text : virtual public node
{
  protected:
    int len;                            // length of array
    char* str;
  // str is used in the same way as an array identifier
  public:
    text( const char* );                     // constructor
    char& operator[ ] ( int i ) { return str[ i ]; }
                        // redefining subscript operator
    void write( ostream& );
                        // redefining virtual function
};
```

```
// class provides for a divider line of i hyphens
class divider : virtual public node
{
   protected:
     int width;                    // field-width of divider
   public:
     divider( int i ) : width( i ){   }
             // using a constructor initialisation list
     void write( ostream& );
                          // redefining virtual function
};

/* class with multiple inheritance, constructor uses
                        both base class constructors */
class header : public text, public divider
{
   public:
     header( const char* s, int i )
                          : text( s ), divider( i ) { }
     void write( ostream& );
                          // redefining virtual function
};
```

11.5.3 The library implementation file

The implementation requires the use of the function, *strlen( )*, from the string library, the function *toupper( )* from the ctype library, and the function *exit( )* from the stdlib library.

The function *toupper( )* is used to put all the alphabetic characters in a **header** array into upper-case.

This final programming example demonstrates *exception handling*. In particular, provision is made for the possibility that the free store has no more storage space available at run-time and so the **new** operator returns null, 0. This exceptional situation may occur, and both libraries and programs should enable some recovery from such a position.

In this library implementation file, and in the program which includes this library, just a simple message is written out and the program is terminated normally using the *exit( )* function.

```
// file page_node

#include <iostream.h>
#include <string.h>
#include <stdlib.h>
#include <ctype.h>
#include "page_node.h"
```

```
/* text constructor is similar to that of myline, in
                      9.5 but with exception handling */
text :: text( const char* s )
{
  len = strlen( s );
  str = new char[ len ];
              // checking for an exceptional possibility
  if ( str == 0 )
    {
      cout << "No more free store available";
      exit( 0 );            // normal program termination
    }
    // free store available, so copy s into free store
  for ( int i = 0; i < len; i++ )
      str[ i ] = s[ i ];
}

/* virtual function redefinition for writing an array of
                      characters to screen or file */
void text :: write( ostream& os )
{
  for ( int i = 0; i < len; i++ )
    os << str[ i ];
  os << endl;
}

/* virtual function redefinition for writing hyphens to
                              screen or file */
void divider :: write( ostream& os )
{
  for ( int i = 0; i < width; i++ )
    os << '-';
  os << endl;
}

/* virtual function redefinition for writing an
   indentation and upper-case text to screen or file */
void header :: write( ostream& os )
{
                      // write indentation as spaces
  for ( int i = 0; i < width; i++ )
    os << ' ';
                      // put text into upper-case letters
  for ( i = 0; i < len; i++ )
    str[ i ] = toupper( str[ i ] );
                              // write text
  for ( i = 0; i < len; i++ )
    os << str[ i ];
  os << endl;
}
```

11.5.4 An insertion-only editor program

This 'editor' program only allows lines of text, horizontal line dividers, and headers to be inserted into a 'page'. It has been kept relatively simple, but demonstrates *exception handling* as well as the handling of a *heterogeneous linked list* using virtual functions and virtual base classes.

There are other possible exceptions that a program may need to check as well as checking that the free store still contains free space. This program allows the user to write out the page to a data file given as the second program argument when the program is run. The function *prog_arg( )* looks at the number of program arguments, **argc,** and terminates the program if only one argument has been given (the first program argument is the executable file name).

```
// file editor
#include <iostream.h>
#include <fstream.h>
#include <stdlib.h>
#include <string.h>
#include "page_node.h"

void prog_arg( int );
            // checks that a data file has been given
void insert_divider( );
void insert_text( );
void insert_header( );
int free_store( node* );
            // checks that free store is still available
void write_page( ostream& );
const LINE_LENGTH = 80;
node* p;      // abstract base class pointer declaration
list page;              // page is a simply linked list

void main( int argc, char* argv[ ] )
{
   prog_arg( argc );
        // if a data file has been given, then continue
   ofstream datafile;
   datafile.open( argv[ 1 ], ios :: out );

   do
    {
        cout << "Give a command:"                 << endl
            << "h    to insert a header"          << endl
            << "t    to insert a line of text"    << endl
            << "d    to insert a divider"         << endl
            << "w    to write out page to screen" << endl
            << "f    to write out page to file"   << endl
            << "q    to quit"                .     << endl
            << "Command given is: ";
```

```
      char command;
      cin >> command; cin.ignore( LINE_LENGTH, '\n' );
      switch ( command)
        {
          case 'h' : insert_header( ); break;
          case 't' : insert_text( ); break;
          case 'd' : insert_divider( ); break;
          case 'w' : write_page( cout ); break;
          case 'f' : write_page( datafile );
        }

    } while ( command != 'q' );

  datafile.close( );
}

// an exception handling function
void prog_arg( int argc )
{
  if ( argc == 1 )
    {
      cout << "Give program argument for data file"
             << endl;
      exit( 0 );
    }
}

void insert_divider( )
{
  int i;
  cout << "Give field-width of divider: ";
  cin >> i;
  p = new divider( i );
  if ( free_store( p ) )
    page.insert( p );
}

void insert_text( )
{
  char buffer[ LINE_LENGTH ], buffer2[ LINE_LENGTH ];
  cout << "Give line of text: " << endl;
  // extraction operator must be used before getline( )
  cin >> buffer;
  cin.getline( buffer2, LINE_LENGTH, '\n' );
  strcat( buffer, buffer2 );        // concatenate input
  p = new text( buffer );
  if ( free_store( p ) )
    page.insert( p );
}
```

```
void insert_header( )
{
    char buffer[ LINE_LENGTH ], buffer2[ LINE_LENGTH ];
    int indent;
    cout << "Give header for page: " << endl;
    cin >> buffer;
    cin.getline( buffer2, LINE_LENGTH, '\n' );
    strcat( buffer, buffer2 );
    cout << "Give indentation required for header: ";
    cin >> indent;
    p = new header( buffer, indent );
    if ( free_store( p ) )
        {
            page.first( );    // insert header at top of page
            page.insert( p );
        }
}

// an exception handling function
int free_store( node* q )
{
    if ( q ) return 1;
            // if p not null then storage available else -
    cout << "No more free store available";
    exit( 0 );
            // no return value needed if program terminates
}

void write_page( ostream& os )
{
    for ( p = page.first( ); p != 0; p = page.next( ) )
        p -> write( os );        // selecting virtual function
}
```

When the program is run, the output could be similar to the following, where film titles were entered alternately with dividers whose given width was '4'; finally, the text for the header *films* was entered with an indentation of '2' and inserted, in upper-case letters, at the top:

```
  FILMS
easy rider
----
jurassic park
----
casablanca
----
```

11.6 Conclusion

With this final program example we can see that C++ has all the attributes of an object-oriented language.

The programmer can define a type, a *class*, needed for an application. A class definition can include constructors so that objects of that class can be declared, and possibly initialised, and can include operator definitions so that such objects can be used in expressions in just the same way as objects of the predefined types.

Further classes can be derived, if required, to form a *hierarchy of classes*, some of which may have *multiple inheritance* from several base classes. Derived classes inherit all the members of a base class, but derived members can be redefined, if necessary.

It is often the case that a required base class can be found in a library that has already been developed. This library may come with the implementation, may be purchased (or be shareware), or may have been developed for a similar application and be found 'in-house'. Such a base class should be reused. *Reusability* is an important consideration in current software development.

In a class hierarchy, it is usually the case that a base class is 'simpler' than a derived class. 'Younger' classes usually have increasing complexity and are oriented towards a specific program requirement.

Finally, this chapter shows that class objects can have differing responses to a message, *polymorphism*, if the message is a virtual function call. The method causing the response is defined by a virtual member function definition given in the class of each object.

Happy programming!

Exercises for Chapter 11

1. Extend the **virt_node** and **page_node** libraries so that instances of objects of the classes derived from class **node** can be read as well as written.

2. Extend the *editor* program to enable the user to be able to read lines from a file into a page, insert lines after a given line, and delete a given line (where the lines may be a **text**, **divider**, or **header** instance).

3. Extend the *editor* program further to enable 'page-breaks'. The user should then be allowed to enter headers which will then be inserted at the top of the current page.

Appendix 1
Using Unix GNU C++ and Borland Turbo C++

Note that Unix and DOS require different *return-types* for the **main** function of a program. These are operating system requirements and both are consistent with C++. If the return-type is not of the type that the operating system is expecting, compilers on both operating systems will give *warnings*, but the program may still be linked and executed if there are no other errors. The example programs in this book all have the return-type **void** required by DOS.

Unix GNU C++

C++ program files have the extension **.cc**. The return-type of the **main( )** function is **integer**. For all the example programs of this book, **void main( )** may be replaced by just **main( )**, the return-type is then implicitly **int**.

After logging in, the prompt given by the operating system is **$** or **%**. The user command lines given below follow the **%** prompt, but they can be used equally well after a **$** prompt.

Entering text

Programs are entered using an editor, this may be *vi* (found on all Unix systems) or *emacs* (found on many Unix systems). If *emacs* is used to enter the program *filename.cc*, the command line to be typed in is:
% emacs filename.cc   // see local documentation on how to use *emacs*

Compiling, linking and running programs

GNU C++ preprocesses, compiles and links both ANSI C and C++ program files. After invoking it with a **gcc** command line we are ready to execute immediately a program if it does not produce any *error* messages (*warning* messages should be carefully considered, and the program only subsequently run if the warning is not a serious one). If error messages do occur, then the syntax of the program should be amended using the editor, and the **gcc** command line entered again.

Unless told otherwise, the **gcc** command will put any executable file that it creates into the file *a.out*. To compile and link *filename.cc* and put the executable file into *a.out*, give the command line:
% gcc filename.cc -lg++
          // compiles & links C++ libraries, and puts executable file into *a.out*

The executable file is then run using:
% a.out

Alternatively, by using the **-o** option, the executable file can be put into any named file *fidentifier*, as in:

% gcc filename.cc   -lg++   -o fidentifier
                               // if successful, the executable file is now *fidentifier*

The executable file is then run using:
% fidentifier

Program arguments

Arguments may be given to a program through the command line; each argument is usually separated by 'white space'. The first argument (argv[0]) is the executable file name as in the command line:

% game2 cities   // argv[0] is *game2* and argv[1] is *cities*

The Unix makefile and the make of a program with user-defined libraries

A **makefile** has to be created (using **emacs** or **vi**) before using the **make** command which will compile and link the files. The **makefile** may contain comments, interdependency information, macro definitions, and executable commands.

The interdependency lines specify how a target file is to be created from a number of files. If these files have been updated more recently than their target file, then the target file will be regenerated according to the commands which follow the dependency line. In its simplest form, a **makefile** has the following format:

```
target : dependency-list
TAB-character executable command
```

Example showing how the *game3* program file can be compiled and linked together with the **mymask** library (discussed in Chapter 6):
Use **emacs** or **vi** to create a **makefile** where the contents of **makefile** are:

```
game3exe: mymask.o game3.o
  gcc mymask.o game3.o  -lg++  -o  game3exe
game3.o:
  gcc  -c  game3.cc  -lg++
mymask.o:
  gcc  -c  mymask.cc  -lg++
```

This **makefile** can then be used, at any time after *game3.cc, mymask.h, mymask.cc* have been entered using **emacs** or **vi**, to produce the executable file *game3exe*, as in:
%make game3exe
    If all is successful, *game3exe* can now be executed using:
%game3exe

Using Borland's Turbo C++ for DOS or DOS + Windows

Turbo C++ program files have the extension *.cpp*.

This is a self-contained program development environment. It contains editing facilities as well as a compiler and a linker that handle both C and C++ files.

Entering text

A window is provided for entering and editing a file. The editor enables simple insertion and deletion at the cursor position, and use of the cursor keys to move around the window. A file may be given a name (or a new name) by using the **File** *Save As* command. More than one editing window may be open during editing sessions - this is particularly useful for developing multi-file programs. The initial editing window will either be a *noname.cpp* file, or your own *filename.cpp* file if you have already retrieved it using the *File Manager*.

Compiling, linking and running programs

When a program file has been entered, it is compiled using the **Compile** *Compile* command producing an object file.

If a program file is successfully compiled, it is then linked and an executable file run using the **Run** *Run* command.

Program arguments

These are entered for a program using **Run** *Arguments*. Note that argv[0] is assumed to be the executable file name and so only argv[1]   argv[2] etc need be entered, each separated by white space.

Using a Project to make and link programs with user-defined libraries

Note that *header files* are **included** within program files (and maybe in one or more implementation files), so they need not be separately compiled or involved in a **make**. However, *implementation files* do need to be compiled before they are linked to a program module.

Enter the **Project** section of the menu given at the top of the screen. Give a **project name**, extension **.prj**. Add the filenames of the program file and the implementation file(s) that you wish to **make** (you can also delete as required). Exit **project**.

After the editor has been used to enter the text of the program file and the library files, ensure that the program is the active file. **make** may be then be used from the **Compile** section of the menu.

If all is successful, you can then run the **project** whenever you wish.

Appendix 2 Escape sequences and ASCII chars

C++ escape sequences, for use within strings (character arrays)

\r CR, carriage return	\n newline (LF line feed & CR)	
\t horizontal tab	\v vertical tab	\f form feed
\' single quote char	\" double quote char	\b backspace
\a bell, alert	\\ backslash char itself	\0 null, string terminator

The American Standard Code for Information Interchange (ASCII) char set

Code	Char	Code	Char	Code	Char	Code	Char
0	Null	32	(space)	64	@	96	'
1	SOH	33	!	65	A	97	a
2	Start text	34	"	66	B	98	b
3	End text	35	#	67	C	99	c
4	EOT	36	$	68	D	100	d
5	ENQ	37	%	69	E	101	e
6	ACK	38	&	70	F	102	f
7	Bell	39	'	71	G	103	g
8	Backspace	40	(	72	H	104	h
9	H. tab	41	)	73	I	105	i
10	LF	42	*	74	J	106	j
11	V. tab	43	+	75	K	107	k
12	Form feed	44	,	76	L	108	l
13	CR	45	-	77	M	109	m
14	SO	46	.	78	N	110	n
15	SI	47	/	79	O	111	o
16	DLE	48	0	80	P	112	p
17	DC1	49	1	81	Q	113	q
18	DC2	50	2	82	R	114	r
19	DC3	51	3	83	S	115	s
20	DC4	52	4	84	T	116	t
21	NAK	53	5	85	U	117	u
22	SYN	54	6	86	V	118	v
23	ETB	55	7	87	W	119	w
24	CAN	56	8	88	X	120	x
25	EM	57	9	89	Y	121	y
26	SUB	58	:	90	Z	122	z
27	ESCape	59	;	91	[	123	{
28	FS	60	<	92	\	124		
29	GS	61	=	93	]	125	}
30	RS	62	>	94	^	126	~
31	US	63	?	95	_	127	DELete

Appendix 3 C++ keywords

All C++ keywords are written in lower case.

asm	delete	if	return	union
auto	do	inline	short	unsigned
break	double	int	signed	virtual
case	else	long	sizeof	void
catch	enum	new	static	volatile
char	extern	operator	struct	while
class	float	private	switch	
const	for	protected	template	
continue	friend	public	this	
default	goto	register	typedef	

Appendix 4 Operator precedence and associativity

The C++ operators grouped in order of decreasing precedence.

Level	Operators	Associativity
1	::	left to right
2	-> . ( ) [ ]	left to right
3	prefix ++ prefix --	right to left
	postfix ++ postfix --	
	~ !	
	unary + unary - unary * unary &	
	(type) sizeof new delete	
4	->* .*	left to right
5	* / %	left to right
6	+ -	left to right
7	<< >>	left to right
8	< <= > >=	left to right
9	== !=	left to right
10	&	left to right
11	^	left to right
12	|	left to right
13	&&	left to right
14	||	left to right
15	?:	left to right
16	= *= /= %= += -=	right to left
	<<= >>= &= ^= |=	
17	,	left to right

Appendix 5 The iostream libraries

Input and output facilities are not defined within the C++ language, but are provided by the **iostream** libraries. A *stream* is an abstraction referring to any flow of data from a source (or producer) to a sink (or consumer). At the lowest level, this is interpreted as the transfer of a sequence of bytes, and there is no concept of the type of the data bytes being handled. At the user level, a stream involves the transfer of a sequence of objects such as characters, integers, etc.

The **iostream** libraries have two parallel families of classes: those derived from **streambuf**, and those derived from **ios**. Both of these base classes are low level classes, and each does a separate set of tasks. All stream classes have at least one of these classes as a base class.

The streambuf classes

The **streambuf** class provides an interface to physical devices. It provides methods for buffering and handling streams when little or no formatting is required. The classes **filebuf** and **strstreambuf** are derived from **streambuf**.

The ios family of classes

The inheritance diagram for the **ios** family, shown on the following page, is not a simple hierarchy because of the generous use of *multiple inheritance* whereby a single class can inherit from more than one base class. *Virtual inheritance*, through the use of *virtual base classes*, avoids multiple declarations. So **fstream**, for instance, inherits members from **ios, istream, ostream, fstreambase,** and **iostream**.

The **ios** class definition includes a pointer member to a **streambuf**. It enables formatted input and output with error-checking using a **streambuf**. All classes in the **ios** family use a **streambuf** (or a **filebuf** or **strstreambuf**, which are special cases of a **streambuf**) as a source and/or sink.

The predefined open streams

The **iostream** class provides four predefined open streams:

```
istream_withassign cin;        // standard input stream, usually keyboard
ostream_withassign cout;       // standard output stream, usually screen
ostream_withassign cerr;       // standard error with unbuffered output
ostream_withassign clog;       // standard error with buffered output
```

ios provides formats for objects of the predefined data types and types derived from these. Users may provide formats for class objects through overloading.

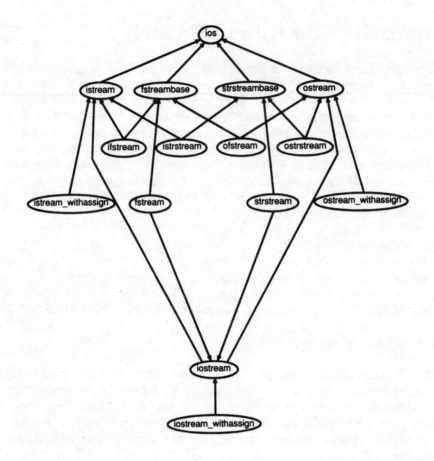

An inheritance diagram for the **ios** family of classes

The extraction operator

Stream input is accomplished with the *extraction* operator >>. Its left operand is an object of class **istream**. The right operand can be of any type or class for which stream input has been defined.

By default, the extraction operator skips whitespace (as defined by the **isspace** function in **ctype.h**), then reads in characters appropriate to the type of the input object until whitespace is again encountered.

The action taken when whitespace is encountered may be altered by using the **ws** manipulator, or by using several **iostream** member functions.

The insertion operator

Stream output is accomplished with the *insertion* operator <<. Its left operand is an object of class **ostream**. Its right operand is an object of any type or class for which stream output has been defined.

The << operator associates from left to right and returns a reference to the **ostream** operator for which it was invoked. This allows insertions to be cascaded in a single statement.

Manipulators

A way to change some of the default format is to use special function-like operators called *manipulators*. These take a stream reference as an argument and return a reference to the same stream. Manipulators can be embedded in a chain of insertions or extractions to alter stream states without actually performing any insertions or extractions. The set of manipulators include:

dec	// set decimal conversion base format
hex	// set hexadecimal conversion base format
oct	// set octal base format
ws	// extract whitespace characters
endl	// insert newline and flush stream
ends	// insert terminal null '\0' in stream
flush	// flush an ostream
setbase(int n)	/* set conversion base format to base n where n is 0, 8, 10, 16, 0 is default giving decimal */
setfill(int c)	// set the fill character to c - default is ' '
setprecision(int n)	// set the float precision to n
setw(int n)	// set the fieldwidth to n

The **iomanip** library enables the manipulators which take arguments. So **iomanip.h** should be included when such manipulators are used.

The input and output libraries

The stream class libraries consists of several classes declared in three header files: **iostream.h, fstream.h,** and **strstream.h.**

Only a selection of detail is given here about classes in the **iostream** and **fstream** libraries.

The iostream library

(i) **class ios**   /* provides operations common to both input and output,
                                           specialising in high-level formatting */
some public member functions:
int bad( );   // nonzero if error occurred
int eof( );   // nonzero on end of file
int fail( );   // nonzero if an operation failed
char fill( );   // returns the current fill character
char fill(char);   // resets the fill character, returns the previous one
int good( );   // nonzero if no errors appeared
int width( );   // returns the current width setting
int width(int);   // sets the width as given; returns the previous width

(ii) **class iostream**   /* inherits from its base classes,
                                  allowing both input and output on a stream */

(iii) **class iostream_withassign**
                              // as **iostream** plus an overloaded assignment operator

(iv) **class istream**   /* provides formatted/ unformatted input
                              >> operator overloaded for all predefined types */
some public member functions:
int gcount( );   // returns the numbers of characters last extracted
int get( );   // extracts the next character or EOF
istream& get(signed char* buffer, int len, char = '\n');
istream& get(unsigned char* buffer, int len, char = '\n');
          /* both of these extract chars into the given buffer until the delimiter
       (third argument) is encountered, or until (**len - 1**) bytes have been read;
     a terminating null '\0' is placed on the char string - the delimiter never is;
                              fails only if no chars were extracted */
istream& get(signed char&);
istream& get(unsigned char&);
              // both of these extract a single char into the given char reference
istream& getline(signed char* buffer, int len, char = '\n');
istream& getline(unsigned char* buffer, int len, char = '\n');
   /* both of these are the same as **get** except that the delimiter is also extracted;
                              the delimiter is not copied to buffer */
istream& ignore(int n = 1, int delim = EOF);
                    /* causes up to n characters in the input stream to be skipped;
                              stops if delim is encountered */
int peek( );   // returns next char without extraction
istream& putback(char);   // pushes back a character into the stream

istream& read(unsigned char*, int);
// extracts a given number of chars into an array
istream& seekg(long);
// moves to an absolute position (as returned from **tellg**)
istream& seekg(long, seek_dir); /* moves to position relative to the current
position, following the definition: **enum seek_dir{ beg, cur, end };** */
long tellg( );   // returns the current stream position

(v) **class istream_withassign**
// is an **istream** with an added assignment operator

(vi) **class ostream**   /* provides formatted and unformatted output
the << operator is overloaded for all the predefined types */
some public member functions:
ostream& flush( );   // flushes the stream
ostream& put(char);   // inserts the char into the output stream
ostream& seekp(long);
// moves to an absolute position (as returned from **tellp**)
ostream& seekp(long, seek_dir); /* moves to position relative to the current
position, following the definition: **enum seek_dir { beg, cur, end }** */
long tellp( );   // returns the current stream position
ostream& write(const unsigned char*, int n);
// inserts n chars (nulls included) into output stream

(vii) **class ostream_withassign**
// is an **ostream** with an added assignment operator

The fstream library

The class of **ofstream** inherits the insertion operations from **ostream**. The class
of **ifstream** inherits the extraction operations from **istream**. The file stream
classes also provide constructors and member functions for creating files and
handling file input and output.

By default, files are opened in text mode. This means that, on input, carriage-
return/linefeed are converted to the '\n' character. On output, the '\n' character
is converted to carriage-return/linefeed.

The file opening mode is set with an optional second argument to the **open**
function, chosen from **ios** constants:

ios :: app   // append data by writing at end of file
ios :: ate   // seek to end of file upon original open
ios :: in   // open for input (default for ifstreams)
ios :: out   // open for output(default for ofstreams)

ios :: binary   // open file in binary mode
ios :: trunc   // discard contents if file exists
ios :: nocreate   // if file does not exist, open fails
ios :: noreplace// if file exists, open for output fails unless *ate* or *app* is set

(i) **class fstream** // provides for simultaneous input and output on a **filebufuf**
constructors:
fstream( );   // makes an **fstream** that is not attached to a file
fstream(const char*, int, int = filebuf :: openprot);
                          // makes an **fstream**, opens a file, and connects to it
fstream(int);   // makes an **fstream**, connects to an open file descriptor
fstream(int, char*, int);
      // makes an **fstream** connected to an open file and uses specified buffer

(ii) **class ifstream**   // provides input operations on a **filebuf**
constructors:
ifstream( );   // makes an **ifstream** that is not attached to a file
ifstream(const char*, int = ios :: in, int = filebuf :: openprot);
                   // makes an **ifstream**, opens an input file in protected mode,
ifstream(int);   // makes an **ifstream**, connects to an open file descriptor
ifstream(int fd, char*, int);
      // makes an **ifstream** connected to an open file and uses specified buffer

(iii) **class ofstream**   // provides input operations on a **filebuf**
constructors:
ofstream( );   // makes an **ofstream** that is not attached to a file
ofstream(const char *, int = ios :: out, int = filebuf :: openprot);
                          // makes an **ofstream**, opens a file, and connects to it
ofstream(int);   // makes an **ofstream**, connects to an open file descriptor

ofstream(int fd, char*, int);
      // makes an **ofstream** connected to an open file and uses specified buffer
public member functions of these **fstream** classes:
void open(const char*, int, int = filebuf :: openprot);
                                              // opens a file for an **fstream**
filebuf* rdbuf( );   // returns the filebuf used
void attach(int);   // connects to an open file descriptor
void close( );   // closes the associated **filebuf** and file
void setbuf(char*, int);   // uses a specified buffer

Appendix 6 Other libraries

The following are some library header file identifiers with a selection of macros and prototypes of functions that are likely to be available together with a C++ compiler. There will be more, many specific to the implementation.

An **int** return type usually indicates that if a function is successful a non-zero (true) value is returned else a zero (false) value is returned. Only when other **int** values are returned are they noted here.

ctype.h   // macros and functions for character testing and conversion

```
int tolower(int ch);
int toupper(int ch);                              /* these convert an integer ch
                      (in the range 0 to 127) to its lowercase/uppercase value,
                                                all others are left unchanged;
            if success, returns converted value, else ch returned unchanged */
int isalnum(int c);                                               /* if success,
                      c is a letter (A to Z or a to z) or a digit (0 to 9) */
int isalpha(int c);              // if success, c is a letter (A to Z or a to z)
int isascii(int c);                                               /* if success,
                          the low order byte of c is in the range 0 to 127 */
int iscntrl(int c);                              /* if success, c is a delete character
                          or ordinary control char in range 0 to 32 */
int isdigit(int c);                      // if success, c is a digit (0 to 9)
int isgraph(int c);                    /* if success, c is a printing character,
            like isprint, except that a space character is excluded */
int islower(int c);                    // if success, c is a lowercase letter (a to z)
int isupper(int c);                    // if success, c is an uppercase letter (A to Z)
int isprint(int c);                    /* if success, c is a printing character,
                                                including space */
int ispunct(int c);                            /* if success, c is a punctuation
                                        character (iscntrl or isspace) */
int isspace(int c);                            /* if success, c is a space, tab,
            carriage return, new line, vertical tab, or formfeed */
```

dir.h   // functions for working with directories

int chdir(const char* path);   /* causes the directory
                    specified by *path* to become the current working directory,
                              path must specify an existing directory */
int mkdir(const char* path);   /* creates a new directory
                                          from the given *path* */
int rmdir(const char* path);   /* deletes the directory
                    given by path; the directory named by path must be empty,
        must not be the current working directory, must not be the root directory */

---

float.h   // macros giving ranges of real number quantities

FLT_DIG   // type float, number of digits of accuracy
FLT_MIN   // type float, minimum value
FLT_MAX   // type float, maximum value
DBL_DIG   // type double, number of digits of accuracy
DBL_MIN   // type double, minimum value
DBL_MAX   // type double, maximum value
LDBL_DIG   // type long double, number of digits of accuracy
LDBL_MIN   // type long double, minimum value
LDBL_MAX   // type long double, maximum value

---

limits.h   // macros giving ranges of integral quantities

CHAR_BIT   // type char, number of bits
CHAR_MAX   // type char, maximum value
CHAR_MIN   // type char, minimum value
INT_MAX   // type int, maximum value
INT_MIN   // type int, minimum value
LONG_MAX   // type long, maximum value
LONG_MIN   // type long, minimum value
SHRT_MAX   // type short, maximum value
SHRT_MIN   // type short, minimum value
UCHAR_MAX   // type unsigned char, maximum value
USHRT_MAX   // type unsigned short, maximum value
UINT_MAX   // type unsigned integer, maximum value
ULONG_MAX   // type unsigned long, maximum value

---

math.h // maths functions

int abs(int x); /* returns the absolute
(positive magnitude) value of an int */
double fabs(double x); // returns the absolute value of a double
int labs(long int x); // returns the absolute value of a long int
double acos(double x); /* returns the arc cosine
of a double in range –1 to 1 */
double asin(double x); /* returns the arc sine
of a double in range –1 to 1 */
double atan(double x); // returns the arc tangent of a double
double ceil(double x); /* rounds up a double;
returns, as a double, the smallest integer not $<$ x */
double floor(double x); /* rounds down a double;
returns, as a double, the largest integer not $>$ x */
double exp(double x); // gives the value e to power x;
double fmod(double x, double y); /* calculates x modulo y,
the remainder of x/y */
double log(double x); // natural logarithm function
double log10(double x); // common logarithm function
double modf(double x, double* ipart); /* splits a **double**
into integer and fraction parts: breaks x into two parts:
the integer and the fraction and stores the integer in *ipart*
and returns the fractional part of x */
double pow(double x, double y); /* power function,
gives x to the power of y (x**y) */
double sqrt(double x); // calculates the positive square root of a double

---

stdlib.h // some commonly used functions

// for program termination
void abort(void); // abnormally terminates a program
void exit(int status); /* provides normal termination,
closing all files and writing buffered output if necessary */

// for random numbers
int rand(void); /* random number generator;
uses a multiplicative congruential random number generator
to return successive pseudo-random numbers in the range 0 to RAND_MAX,
returns the generated pseudo-random number */
void srand(unsigned seed); /* initialises random number generator;
the generator is set to a new starting point with each seed number */

// for searching and sorting
void* bsearch(const void* key, const void* base, size_t nelem, size_t width,
    int (*fcmp)(const void*, const void*)); /* performs a binary search
on a sorted list of data objects: makes a binary search for the value *key in a
table (array) of **nelem** elements in memory where **base** is the base (0th element)
of the search table, **fcmp** is a user-defined comparison routine that compares two
items and returns a value based on the comparison, **key** is the item to be searched
for (the search key), **nelem** is the number of entries in the table, **width** is the
number of bytes in each entry; on success returns address of the first matching
item in the table else returns 0 */

void qsort(void* base, size_t nelem, size_t width, int (*fcmp)(const void* ,
    const void*)); /* sorts using the quicksort algorithm
(is an implementation of the "median of three" variant of the quicksort algorithm)
where **base** is the base (0th element) of the search table, **fcmp** is a user-defined
comparison routine that compares two items and returns a value based on the
comparison, **nelem** is the number of entries in the table, **width** is the number of
bytes in each entry; returns no value */

---

string.h   // functions for handling char arrays terminating with '\0'

char* strcat(char* dest, const char* src); /* appends a copy of src
                to the end of dest, the length of the resulting string is
    strlen(dest) + *strlen(src)*; returns a pointer to the concatenated strings */
char* strchr(const char* s, int c); /* scans a string s
                for the first occurrence of char c; if success,
        returns a pointer to the first occurrence of the char else returns null */
int strcmp(const char* s1, const char*s2); /* compares two strings
    from the first character in each string until the corresponding chars differ
                or until the end of the strings is reached; returns an int value
    that is: < 0 if s1 < s2 , == 0 if s1 == s2 , > 0 if s1 > s2 */
char* strcpy(char* dest, const char* src); /* copies string src to dest;
                returns pointer to dest */
int strlen(const char* s); /* calculates length of a string;
    returns the number of characters in s, not counting the terminating null */
char* strstr(const char* s1, const char* s2); /* finds the first occurrence
                of string s2 in string s1; if success
        returns a pointer to the char in s1 where s2 begins else returns null */
char* strpbrk(const char* s1, const char* s2); /* scans a string, s1,
                for the first occurrence of any char appearing in s2; if success
        returns a pointer to the first occurrence a char in s2 else returns null */

Index